WINNING

at

RETIREMENT

*A Guide to Health, Wealth, & Purpose
in the Best Years of Your Life*

Patrick Foley, CFP®

Kristin Hillsley

ISBN-13: 978-0-692-19789-9

www.RetiredHappy.me

For more information, contact Patrick Foley

at pfoley@rwbaird.com or (610)238-6637.

Contents

Introduction

If you are in retirement, or are starting to look forward to it, we have some good news for you: turns out the peak ages for happiness are later in life. In fact, people are more likely to describe themselves as "very happy" at 69 than at any other age.[1] One study[2] found that just under half of retirees describe themselves as "very satisfied" in retirement. Not bad odds—although the number was above 60% back in 1998, so the trend is not looking good. If about half of retirees describe themselves as very satisfied and half do not, the question is . . . how do you end up in the "winning" half?

That's the question we set out to answer, and our findings are described in this book. The title is tongue-in-cheek, of course. Retirement is not a game to be played, nor a contest. But we want you to get fired up about it. You should be excited about retirement; you should view it as a great opportunity and a grand adventure. Our search for answers about retirement happiness was enlightening and filled us with optimism. We discovered common elements that seem to put people on the right path, and all should be within your grasp.

Retirement is a blank sheet of paper. It is a chance to redesign your life into something new and different. For many, that something proves to be a lifestyle characterized by freedom and happiness . . . the best of times, the golden age. We are here to provide you with advice that will maximize your chances of crafting that sort of retirement for yourself.

••

TED Talks

One way wisdom is shared these days is through TED Talks (and related TEDx Talks). Short for "Technology, Entertainment and Design," these are brief presentations that allow some of the most brilliant minds in the world to share their thoughts and theories. We will discuss TED Talks in greater detail in Chapter 8: Tech Tools for Retirement Success. Until then, look for TED callout boxes throughout the book referencing presentations related to the content we will cover. You can visit TED.com and search the title of a talk to find it, or if you search for the title on Google, you should find it hosted on YouTube.

••

Turning Points

There are several natural turning points that happen in life. Not every person experiences every one of them, and life has a way of throwing unexpected changes at us—good and bad—that do not fit into these neat little boxes. But there are some common transitions that most people encounter. Each is an opportunity for reinvention.

There is the transition from grade school to high school, and (for some) from high school to college. When you switch schools, especially if it involves moving or being surrounded by a different group of kids, it is a chance to become a new person to a certain extent. You could end up with different friends, develop new interests, maybe change your hair or style of dress. Going to a new school can represent a major identity shift. Most of the time we carry over a good deal of our prior persona, but there is at least the option of a fresh start.

After school the next big change is finding a "real" job. The career choice. For some this will be the first step down a fairly straight path. For others, the beginning of a winding road. In any case, choosing a career is a defining moment. After all, so much of who we are in life is based on the work that we do.

Marriage is another momentous life change. Choose right, and it might be the most positive decision you ever make. The life turn that will shape everything that follows for the better. Choose wrong, and all manner of mayhem can ensue. There is a vast spectrum of marriage outcomes ranging from something out of a romance novel to the John and Lorena Bobbitt story. No matter what happens, marriage represents a big-time life transition.

And then, for some people, there are children. Wow, there's a transition! This is the change that you have the least amount of control over. It is no longer just you (and your spouse) calling the shots. Oh no, your life is now dictated by one or several part-time maniacs called children. Of course, for many, this is the most fulfilling of life's transitions. Parenthood can provide meaning to your life. For a hectic period of years, and in some ways forever, your existence will be shaped dramatically by your role as a parent if you end up on that path.

The Golden Years

The last common turning point is retirement. This change often comes less encumbered than those that came before it. It can be, as we said, a blank sheet of paper. It is our intent to give you some ideas that will help you navigate that blank sheet. But first, let's start with some great news: there is a strong chance that retirement will represent the best time of your life. Yes, that is the incredible, surprising, uplifting reality of retirement. According to the data we've seen, for a large number of people, retirement rocks.

A variety of studies and surveys depict happiness trends at different ages as being U-shaped. On average, happiness is high in our late teens and early twenties, then trends down until it hits a low point between the ages of 50 and 53. But then there is a shift and happiness begins to rise into retirement and beyond, eventually hitting the highest levels in our 70s and beyond. Shocker, right? Well, perhaps not if you are already there, and have experienced this phenomenon for yourself.

Figure I.1: The Happiness Curve

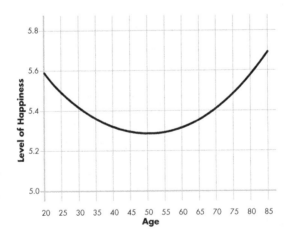

From **The Happiness Curve**, © Jonathan Rauch.
Reprinted by permission.

Let's consider the happiness curve in light of the big life transitions we just talked about. Although then we'll talk about the fact that biology may play a role as well.

Youth is a time for infinite optimism. Every kid is going to be an astronaut, right? And in our teens and early 20s, we tend to be possessed of a sense of immortality and—hopefully—belief in a boundless future.

With the end of adolescence, optimism may be harder to come by. Your mid- to late 20s are a time of new personal freedom as you leave school behind and try to embark on a career path. But it can be a time of too much freedom; you might not have a sense of direction yet. Financial security is probably a distant dream at this point, and chances are you can't really answer the question: "What do you want to do with the rest of your life?"

As you move into marriage and, especially, parenthood, the pressures of becoming a real grown-up can become acute. During these times, as we struggle with a wide variety of stresses, happiness can be elusive. And looking forward might not provide much help, as we see retirement as either something abstract, something vaguely comical (shuffleboard and early-bird specials), or something to dread.

Thankfully, we are probably looking at it all wrong. As the data referenced earlier shows, the best years may still lie ahead. This idea might run counter to what you have been thinking about retirement, and aging in general, for most of your life. In our youth-obsessed culture it is common to dread retirement. Let's face it: no one is excited about aging. The last birthday anyone looks forward to is 21; after that we tend to view the passing of the years with some measure of concern, regret, or outright terror. It's hard not to equate aging with death, and during the various stages of our youth, retirement is associated with physical decline and proximity to the end.

We will look at the critical subject of health and wellness later on, because warding off physical decline is key to a successful retirement. In any case, the big secret that many in retirement know is that, despite the obvious challenges presented by aging, our later years can still turn out to be our best years.

While researching this book we set out to read everything we could get our hands on related to the central idea of finding happiness in retirement. We came across a number of great books in the process, and you'll find them all listed on the Library page[3] of RetiredHappy.me (the companion website for this book, which contains additional resources related to the topics we will cover). We discovered one example—*The Happiness Curve: Why Life Gets Better After Midlife*[4] —as we were putting the finishing touches on this book.

The Happiness Curve was so compelling that it caused us to rewrite the section you are reading right now. Primarily because we got something wrong: we thought that the U-shaped curve of happiness was entirely a function of life circumstances. Instead, it turns out that we may be hardwired for a dose of misery in our 40s and 50s, followed by rising happiness into our later years. In fact, the pattern has even been detected in studies of monkeys.

The implications of this information are significant, especially for anyone in their 40s and 50s who may be feeling a gnawing sense of depression or discontent. Turns out the concept of "midlife crisis" might be missing the mark. A better description for a large number of people might be "midlife malaise." And there may actually be some sort of biological imperative causing people to feel blue in midlife.

The good news is that the tide tends to reverse, and many of us can look forward to brighter days ahead. In fact, the research suggests that our days grow and stay brighter until much later in life (well into our 80s), when health issues often become a big factor.

Obviously the concept is all about averages, and not everyone will experience the same pattern. Also, life can throw curve balls at us that interfere with this natural uptrend in happiness. Nonetheless, it's an optimistic and encouraging concept, and it is well supported by scientific data. We recommend *The Happiness Curve* enthusiastically for adults of all ages, as this seems like a critical concept for people to understand as they make their way through life's changes and challenges.

A Vision of the Future

Throughout this book, we are going to focus on describing specific attitudes and action steps that we hope will increase your chances for happiness in retirement, but let's take a minute to think about the world you will retire into. We have no way of knowing what the future will look like exactly. But it might be a constructive exercise to engage in a bit of futurism and imagine the good and bad that may lie ahead.

Let's start with the bad. After all, we are so bombarded with negativity these days that it sometimes seems like there is nothing else.

Anyone old enough to be seriously contemplating retirement can remember the sense of constant looming threat that America lived with during the Cold War. Depending on your age, this may conjure images of the Vietnam War, the Cuban Missile Crisis, or drills during school where they taught you to hide under your desk in case of a nuclear attack (a plan surely dreamed up by government committee). But then, seemingly out of the blue, the Soviet Union crumbled, the Berlin Wall fell, and for an all-too-brief period there was a time of relative peace in the world.

Then came 9/11 and everything changed again. Or, in a sense, returned to the way things had been. Once again there is the looming threat, the fear that slips from our mind for a bit, but is brought back to the fore again and again by news of war, terror attacks, threats, and a world in turmoil.

But hey, at least that stuff keeps our minds off the national debt. Having barely survived the financial crisis of 2008—a modern economic meltdown rivaled only by the Great Depression in terms of impact—we can add a sense of economic dread to our fears of war and terrorism. Faith in our politicians is plumbing new lows as the reality of the societal problems we face is matched with a feeling that our leaders lack either the ideas or the fortitude needed to solve them. The nightly news is filled with debate about the economic viability of the Social Security and healthcare systems. Our population is aging—a problem shared by much of the developed world—which strains the resources needed to support happy, healthy retirements.

On top of all that, there is growing concern about the proliferation of technology and what that might mean for the future. As more and more tasks can be automated and handled by computers or robots, where does that leave humans? Will we need to reshape our economic system to accommodate a more automated world? Will the gap between rich and poor continue to grow, and with it political instability? Or more frightening still, will technological tools of destruction—such as nuclear and biological weapons—lead to a horrific outcome at some point down the road?

On the other hand, by most metrics human beings have it far better today than at any point in history. A book called *Abundance*[5] by Peter Diamandis highlights the tremendous advantages provided by technological advancement, and describes potential benefits that may lie ahead. Diamandis quotes NYU's Dr. Marc Siegel on our current state of relative prosperity:

> **TEDx Talk**
>
> *David Autor — Will automation take away all our jobs?*
>
> Conventional wisdom these days is that robots are going to take all of our jobs. But Autor discusses the fact that history has shown labor force participation has increased over time as automation has risen.

"Statistically, the industrialized world has never been safer. Many of us are living longer and more uneventfully. Nevertheless, we live in worst-case fear scenarios. Over the past century, we Americans have dramatically reduced our risk in virtually every area of life, resulting in life spans 60 percent longer in 2000 than in 1900. Antibiotics have reduced the likelihood of dying from infections .... Public health measures dictate standards for drinkable water and breathable air. Our garbage is removed quickly. We live in temperature-controlled, disease-controlled lives. And yet, we worry more than ever before. The natural dangers are no longer there, but the response mechanisms are still in place, and now they are turned on much of the time. We implode, turning our adaptive fear mechanism into a maladaptive panicked response."

We recommend checking out *Abundance* because, in addition to being a smart and entertaining read, it provides a welcome dose of optimism in a world that seems beset by negativity and stress. Specifically, it describes advancements in farming, healthcare, and the availability of clean water that could lead to unprecedented improvements in living conditions in the developing world, which in turn could lessen the global want that foments problems like war and terrorism. *Factfulness: Ten Reasons We're Wrong About the World—and Why Things Are Better Than You Think*[6] is another book that paints an optimistic picture (with data), while explaining why we are predisposed to see more negativity than positivity in the world.

As to the problem of automation replacing jobs, economist David Autor argues that this is an age-old concern that never seems to be borne out in reality. For example, he notes that in the decades since automated teller machines came into wide use, the number of bank teller jobs has actually doubled. And while farming and manufacturing jobs have decreased, a whole slew of careers in fields like computers and healthcare have taken their place. Essentially, as technology takes away some jobs and increases productivity, new job demand is created (often in forms of work that would never have been envisioned at the time of the initial technological disruption). Autor does worry that low-paying and high-paying jobs are experiencing growth, while mid-level jobs are being displaced, but he argues that a more effective approach to education—making more of our population suited to higher wage work—could provide a solution.

Another aspect of technological development that bears watching for retirees is automated driving. At the time of this writing, a division of Google called Waymo has a fleet of driverless cabs in active testing.

Dozens of other companies, ranging from leading automakers and tech firms to startups, are competing to own a piece of this potentially transformational space. Many billions of dollars have already been invested, and it's all moving so fast that from the time we wrote the first draft of this chapter until the time we were ready to go to print about a year and a half later, we needed to rewrite this part of it.

Currently, all major automakers have some form of automated driving technology in the works, with many pointing to 2021 for the availability of "level 5" automation . . . where the cars are fully self-driving and wouldn't even need to be equipped with steering wheels (Waymo is at that level now on a limited basis). How quickly this technology will develop and proliferate is a matter of great debate, but it is coming. This will likely represent a huge technological disruption that will cause some job losses (cab and truck drivers), while potentially impacting where people live, where they vacation, the delivery of goods and services, the insurance industry, and much more.

Think of automated driving from the perspective of aging, however, and the implications are exciting. Mobility is a challenge later in life. When someone should give up the car keys is a difficult question faced by many a retiree, and—often with great difficulty—their families. But what if there were no keys to give up? What if you could affordably summon an automated car anytime you'd like, with the press of a button on your phone? This is not science fiction; this will be our reality in the years ahead. For older retirees it would mean less of a struggle getting to doctor appointments or running errands. It could mean the ability to vacation farther away, or even live farther away while maintaining the ability to easily visit family. This technology could represent a tremendous, liberating boon for retirees in the years to come.

It's impossible to predict all the challenges (and positive developments) that we will encounter in the future. But in confronting the difficulties and threats of our time, we would do well to remember that human beings have always been beset by difficulties and threats. In fact, by almost any objective measure we are blessed to live better now, on average, than in any other period in history. Humankind, and America, have faced incredible challenges in the past and have always found a way to overcome and move forward. We should remain optimistic that we will find a way to meet the challenges of the future as well . . . because it does us little good to think otherwise. In seeking a path toward retirement happiness, what benefit is there to wallowing in negative assumptions? In fact, as we will discuss in Chapter 7, taking an optimistic view of life may actually help extend it.

If you are really unhappy with the vision of the world that you perceive before you, then maybe your mission in retirement should be to find a way to change things for the better in whatever way you can (see Chapter 1: A Life of Purpose).

Purpose + Security + Wellness = Happiness

There is a ton of information available about finding happiness later in life, including great books, studies, articles, and websites. It is impossible to fully cover every subject related to retirement in a single book, so in many cases we will point you in the direction of other resources that will help you to take a deeper dive into a topic.

We will summarize all that we have learned about this vast subject, and break it down to a few key areas of focus.

Our research on retirement found that the same themes, presented in varying verbiage and data, kept coming through. Happiness in retirement is possible, even likely. To achieve it you need to do three things:

- Live guided by a **sense of purpose:** We urge you to spend some time thinking about how you intend to live your life in retirement, and what your purpose will be. Have you ever pondered the question: "If I could go back in time and give my younger self advice, what would it be?" Forget that—it doesn't do you any good. Instead, give the current you some good advice. What can you do right now that will change the rest of your days for the better? That is what we are here to talk about.

- Maintain a degree of **financial stability and security** (although it is possible to find happiness with a lot of money or a little).

- **Work consistently on your physical and mental wellness.**

If you pull together all three of those elements—and we are here to help you do that—you will greatly increase your chances of ending up happy or, put another way, of winning at retirement. In the remaining chapters of this book, you will be given advice on how to expand your knowledge by leveraging the internet and other modern tools that are reshaping what is possible for today's retirees. In the end, we'll provide a clear series of steps that can help you end up among the happy half of retired Americans.

We hope that you enjoy this book, and that you come away with answers and ideas that put you firmly on the path to that goal.

> **TED Talk**
>
> *Dan Gilbert—The surprising science of happiness.*
>
> Turns out, happiness may have much more to do with the way we process information than with things that happen to us.

Endnotes

1   Is happiness just a matter of waiting for the right age? https://www.brookings.edu/blog/future-development/2015/11/09/is-happiness-just-a-matter-of-waiting-for-the-right-age/

2   Trends in Retirement Satisfaction in the United States: Fewer Having a Great Time. https://www.ebri.org/pdf/notespdf/EBRI_Notes_04_Apr16.Ret-Satis.pdf

3   https://retiredhappy.me/books-page/

4   *The Happiness Curve: Why Life Gets Better After Midlife* by Jonathan Rauch. ISBN-13: 978-1472960986

5   *Abundance: The Future Is Better Than You Think* by Peter H. Diamandis. ISBN-13: 978-1451616835

6   *Factfulness: Ten Reasons We're Wrong About the World—and Why Things Are Better Than You Think* by Hans Rosling. ISBN-13: 978-1250107817

CHAPTER 1

A Life of Purpose

Most people know they need to approach retirement with some sort of plan for their finances and their healthcare. But for some reason few bother to plan for the rest of it: how they are going to spend their time, what they want to accomplish, the relationships they want to build and maintain with others. It is this "rest of it" that really matters. Saving money and staying healthy are things we do in order to be able to live the lifestyle we want. But are we giving enough thought to what that lifestyle is going to be? What will make us happy? What will keep our hearts and minds engaged?

In short, **what will give life a sense of purpose?** It is a question we should ask ourselves throughout life, but it takes on a different dynamic in retirement. In part because retirees have an abundance of free time, and in part because for many people setting aside their career represents a significant loss of purpose, one that needs to be replaced to keep us feeling engaged in life.

We should also consider that later in life it is hard to escape the reality that the "clock is ticking." With a limited amount of years or (ideally) decades left, do you want to spend most of the time sitting on a couch watching TV? Hopefully you want much more out of retirement. Wanting much more, and seeking it out, will likely have a big impact on your happiness in this period of life. It is easy to imagine why a life of purpose would be fulfilling. But beyond the abstract appeal, there is evidence that remaining highly engaged and goal-oriented in retirement can have profound health benefits.[1]

Purpose is a complicated concept. To start with, it is about meaning and motivation. What is important to you? What are your beliefs? Why do you get out of bed in the morning? What will keep you getting out of bed—or better yet, *springing* out of bed—in your retirement years? It could be a quest for knowledge, a business venture, spending time with your grandchildren, giving back to your community, or a beautiful mix of those or other pursuits.

Beyond motivation, there is the related idea of identity. Who do you see yourself as in retirement? How will other people see you?

As you plan for retirement, you need to contemplate not just **how you will spend your time** but also what your motivations will be. Spend some time pondering your retirement identity. What you do and why you do it combine to define your purpose. In the final chapter ("The Retirement Happiness Map"), we will walk you through some exercises that will include addressing those philosophical topics, along with the more practical matters we will cover in other chapters.

"Cheer up. Your life isn't meaningless.
God put you on this earth for a purpose...
to buy dog food and clean up after me."

A Higher Calling

Are you passionate about politics, or a charitable endeavor? Is there a disease that you want to help conquer? Is there an organization that played a big role in your life that you'd like to give back to? Are you a person of faith for whom belief, and your church and its community, are of highest importance? What we are asking about here are your values, things that move you to the core.

We have a client who recently retired from running a charity dedicated to providing scholarships to underprivileged children, who will continue her mission as an education consultant in retirement. A client couple in their mid-70s participate with their church in educational efforts in Africa. Others serve on charitable boards, or are otherwise active in philanthropy. They may even be helping their own health while helping others . . . a University of Michigan study determined that volunteering correlated to a significantly lower chance of dying over a seven-year period.[2] Truly a win-win!

When thinking of your purpose in retirement, start with your values. Mixed in with all the fun you should be having, consider spending time doing something aligned with your values. Whether a lofty and time-consuming effort, or something on a smaller scale, give back in some way. Your life will be richer and more rewarding for it . . . and maybe healthier as well.

Retirement Lifestyle Books

In our research we came across two great books that focus on the idea of finding purpose in retirement: *The New Retirementality*,[3] and *How to*

Retire Happy, Wild, and Free.[4] Both warn of the risk of idleness or lack of purpose, although each leans in a different direction when offering a solution.

The New Retirementality espouses the benefits of continuing some form of work in retirement. It could be a part-time or consulting extension of your former career, an entirely new career, volunteering, or entrepreneurism. This theme dovetails with statistics showing that more and more people are choosing to work beyond retirement,[5] sometimes after taking a small break before "unretiring."

TED Talk:

Robert Waldinger — What makes a good life? Lessons from the longest study on happiness.

An 80-year study of 724 men from all walks of life found that loneliness is toxic, and that remaining socially connected is a key factor in happiness.

The New Retirementality seems to suggest that if you aren't careful, retirement can kill you. In fact, we initially gave some thought to calling this book "Retirement Can Kill You: A Survival Guide." But aside from finding that the phrase "Survival Guide" had already been used for a book from AARP, we soon realized that the title was much too pessimistic for what turns out to be such an optimistic subject.

In any case, *The New Retirementality* warns of "the four Ds and big B of retirement":

- Death

- Divorce

- Disability

- Drunkenness

- Boredom

In fact, the book even points out the risk in that most quintessential of retirement pursuits: golf. Many of us conjure visions of golf courses in retirement, even metaphorically if we don't actually play golf. But while golf can involve walking, being with friends, and getting out into the sunshine and fresh air, it often ends with drinks at the bar and at best can fill only part of a day. Ultimately, with apologies to the wannabe Jack Nicklauses out there, it's hard to call golf a "purpose" in life. Even if you love it, a life of golf alone is likely to lead to boredom. And as so perfectly described in *The New Retirementality*: "First you are bored, then you are boring."

To Work or Not to Work?

While *The New Retirementality* urges you to work (in some form) forever, *How to Retire Happy, Wild, and Free* seems to lean in the opposite direction. A general theme of this wise and enjoyable book is that you should get out of the rat race as soon as possible. The seemingly competing themes of these books—work forever or stop working as soon as possible—are not as contradictory as they may seem at first glance. The underlying idea in each case is to pursue something that will give you enjoyment and a sense of purpose, and by extension, will bring you happiness. *The New Retirementality* puts emphasis on extending or reinventing your career in retirement, while *How to Retire Happy, Wild, and Free* emphasizes "non-work" pursuits like charitable efforts and continuing education.

The bottom line—and we encourage you to read both books for a deeper dive into the concept—is that to maximize your chance of retirement bliss, you need to come up with a purpose for your life. Purpose comes in many different forms (freedom is the real beauty of retirement), but you should have a mission of sorts, a passion to pursue.

The Perfect Entrepreneur

Now let's talk about the possibility of pursuing that crazy business idea you have been mulling over. Or if you haven't been mulling over a crazy business idea, let's talk about why you might want to start. There are two primary impediments to starting a business: fear and lack of capital. If you have done a good job of saving for retirement, you may have already overcome the latter problem. As far as fear, assuming you are smart about how much you can put at risk, that might not be a major problem either. After all, you (hopefully) no longer have to worry about supporting a family, or setting money aside for college, or saving for retirement, or even maintaining a certain social image. If you have managed to retire "happy, wild, and free," then you have little to lose, as long as you do not risk the money you need to live on.

In business there is the concept of working capital, which is the amount of money required to keep the operation running. Anything above that can either be reinvested or distributed to investors as dividends. What if we look at retirement the same way? Working capital is the amount of money you need to sustain your lifestyle (we will explore finances in detail in Chapter 3: Five Money Maxims, and Chapter 4: Managing Your Nest Egg). Excess capital is money you can either distribute—to family or to charities—or that you can reinvest.

Reinvestment can happen in your traditional investment portfolio . . . but it can also happen by starting a new business venture.

It is easier than ever before to start a business. In the old days you needed to come up with a product, figure out a way to manufacture it, rent space for a store to sell it from, and then create an advertising plan so that you could convince people to buy it. Now, aside from "come up with a product (or service)," the rest can be done relatively easily on the internet. We don't mean to suggest that creating a successful business is easy . . . just that getting one off the ground is not terribly hard these days.

There are many resources available that teach you how to start an online business. There are books that cover the subject in detail such as *Launch: An Internet Millionaire's Secret Formula to Sell Almost Anything Online, Build a Business You Love, and Live The Life of Your Dreams.*[6] We will discuss using the internet effectively to research all manner of topics—whether starting a business, staying fit, or finding a great place to live—in Chapter 8: Tech Tools for Retirement Success.

In addition to information about the nuts and bolts of starting a business, the internet is full of ideas and inspiration for budding entrepreneurs. In fact, an entire ecosystem born of Silicon Valley has been built around the idea of thinking big and being creative. Tim Ferriss is something of a guru in this space, and his blog and books like *The 4-Hour Workweek* are good ways to get introduced to this world of inspiration.

If you have ever dreamed of being an entrepreneur, maybe now is the time to put that dream into action. It can fill your day, give you a sense of purpose and identity, and perhaps even make you some money.

Who Are You in Retirement?

Have you ever met someone who recounts in painful detail every shot of their round of golf? Or worse, every painful detail of their aches and pains? Don't be that person! Prior to retirement, most people describe themselves by what they do. *I am a teacher* . . . *I am a student* . . . *I am a financial advisor* . . . *I am a homemaker*, and so forth.

Who are you in retirement? "I am retired" is a vague statement that is appropriate to the blank-slate nature of post-work life. But think of how much more interesting you will be if you can answer, "I'm retired and spending lots of time with my grandchildren," or "I'm retired but volunteer three days a week at a homeless shelter," or "I retired as a teacher several years ago and then I started my own business."

It is up to you to define who you are in retirement, what your purpose in life is. No one else can do this work for you. It's important, if for no other reason than to give you something to talk about other than missing a putt or bursitis!

Endnotes

1   Effects of Purpose in Life on the Relation Between Alzheimer's Disease Patho-logical Changes on Cognitive Function in Advanced Age. https://www.ncbi.nlm.nih.gov/pmc/articles/PMC3389510/

2   Volunteering and Mortality Among Older Adults: Findings From a National Sample. https://pdfs.semanticscholar.org/09f0/f3daceb8c7d21aa219437d-3de92bfec7ea07.pdf

3   *The New Retirementality: Planning Your Life and Living Your Dreams... at Any Age You Want* by Mitch Anthony. ISBN-13: 978-1118705124

4   *How to Retire Happy, Wild, and Free: Retirement Wisdom That You Won't Get from Your Financial Advisor* by Ernie J. Zelinski. ISBN-13: 978-0969419495

5   Take This Job and Love It! https://www.aarp.org/work/working-after-retire-ment/info-2015/work-over-retirement-happiness.html

6   *Launch: An Internet Millionaire's Secret Formula to Sell Almost Anything Online, Build a Business You Love, and Live The Life of Your Dreams* by Jeff Walker. ISBN-13: 978-1630470173

CHAPTER 2

A Game Plan for Social Security

No matter whether they have $1 or $1,000,000 saved for retirement, most people in the United States qualify for (and rely on) Social Security benefits. That's why we are going to begin our discussion of money by focusing on what is, admittedly, a boring, boring topic, chock-full of numbers and complex rules. You can't talk retirement without talking Social Security. It is a critical subject for retirees in America.

For most retirees, Social Security provides the bulk of their income. For many, it is the only thing separating them from a life of poverty.[1] For others, it is a reliable foundation for meeting necessary expenses so that other monies can be spent on lifestyle choice. Either way, for almost everyone, it is a key element of the lifetime income plan.

In your epic quest for retirement happiness, one of the biggest decisions you will face is when to "turn on" (start collecting) your Social Security income. This is called your **claiming strategy.** Here is the simplified version: barring some exceptions, you will turn on your Social Security benefits sometime between ages 62 and 70, and the longer you wait the higher your monthly income will be.

From there it gets complicated. There are many variables involved and some guesswork. Ultimately the decision boils down to a bet on life expectancy. If you knew exactly how long you—and your spouse if you are married—were going to live, it would be fairly easy to figure out when to turn on your income (as we'll explain later in this chapter).

But since no one has that information, deciding when to activate Social Security income becomes an educated guess. We will provide the "educated" part by describing the variables involved and how they change the odds. After that, the guess is up to you.

The Basics

In 1937 Ernest Ackerman received a lump sum payment of 17 cents from the U.S. government, and the Social Security system was born. A few years later, Ida May Fuller received her first monthly check of $22.54 and the program of monthly income as we know it today began.

The Social Security system provides a variety of benefits:

- Monthly retirement income

- Spousal benefits

- Survivor benefits

- Disability income

- Dependent benefits

- Child benefits

- A $255 death benefit

The right to receive retirement benefits is based on credits, which you get by working (and paying Social Security taxes). The level of income you need to earn a credit varies from year to year. For 2018 it's one credit for each $1,320 of income. The max you can accumulate is four credits per year. So if you earn at least $5,280 in a year, you get four credits. Once you have accumulated 40 credits, you are eligible to receive Social Security benefits. To put it simply: you need to work for 10 years, at a fairly low level of income, to become eligible for Social Security. Certain limitations apply in the case of railroad workers and those who receive government pensions.

••
Maximum benefits

There is a limit to the total amount of income that a family—worker, spouse, children, and dependent parents— can receive based on one worker's income. Typically the cap is 150%–180% of the amount the worker receives (the limit does not apply to divorced spouses). Higher amounts can be earned if both spouses worked and qualify for Social Security.

••

Full Retirement Age (FRA) is a key date for Social Security income calculations, and ranges between 65 and 67 years old, depending on your birth year. People born prior to 1938 had an FRA of 65. That number adjusts higher with later birth dates, and maxes out at 67 for those born after 1959. FRA is not scheduled to rise any higher than 67 at the moment, but as we will discuss later changes to the system are likely at some point.

You receive your full income benefit at FRA. Your monthly retirement income is reduced if you turn it on prior to then, and is increased if you wait until later (it maxes out at age 70). A number of other aspects of the Social Security benefits we will discuss are calculated in relation to FRA. For purposes of simplicity, in this book we will generally assume (unless otherwise noted) a full retirement age of 66.

....

The impact of collecting benefits before FRA while still working

If you have not yet reached FRA and continue to work while receiving Social Security, a portion—either half or a third of it, depending on your age—will be deferred until you reach FRA. Because of the deferral, and the fact that your monthly benefits will be **permanently** reduced due to turning on early, you should think twice about taking benefits while working prior to FRA. Beyond FRA you can work and none of your benefits will be withheld.

....

The more you earn during your working years, the more income you will receive in retirement. The Social Security Administration calculates the payments by taking an average of your 35 highest-earning years. If you work less than 35 years, your average will include zeros for the years you did not work.

In 2018 the maximum level of earned income included in the calculation is $128,400. Visit www.ssa.gov/planners/maxtax.html for a chart of maximum income levels for various years. If you can put together 35 years of earnings at or above the maximum annual level, you will receive the maximum amount of monthly income. In 2018, the maximum income for an individual was $2,788 at FRA or $3,698 for those who wait until age 70.[2] However, the average benefit per 2017 data is $1,360/month ($2,260 for a couple).

As you approach age 62, you need to decide when to turn on your income for yourself if you are single, and if you are married, in coordination with the income of your spouse. Married couples need to consider what will happen upon the death of a spouse. Divorce has certain implications as well. (These topics are addressed later in this chapter.)

Given our focus on retirement, we will not cover income for dependent children or disability income (although these can certainly be relevant for some retirees). For a comprehensive overview of the Social Security system including those subjects, we refer you to ssa.gov, the official site of the Social Security Administration. It is fairly easy to navigate, and provides a wealth of information on the topic.

In the rest of this chapter, we'll talk about *how* to turn on your benefits, discuss *when* to turn them on (for singles and for couples), and address some other common questions about Social Security.

What Have You Qualified For and How Can You Collect?

How much can you expect to receive from Social Security? After age 60 you will receive a printed copy of your Social Security statement in the mail each year, which provides estimates of the income you will receive. Prior to age 60 you can obtain a statement online at www.ssa.gov/mystatement.

If you do not have a recent Social Security statement, visit ssa.gov and click the "My Social Security" button to either create or access your account. Once you are logged on, you can download a statement, where you will find a summary that should look something like Figure 2.1 (we've highlighted in bold the figures to focus on):

Figure 2.1: Your Estimated Benefits Sample Statement

Your Estimated Benefits

*Retirement   You have earned enough credits to qualify for benefits. At your current earnings rate, if you continue working until...

your full retirement age (67 years), your payment would be about. . **$ 2,908** a month

age 70, your payment would be about.........................**$ 3,610** a month

age 62, your pay1nent would be about ....**$ 2,000** a month

*Disability   You have earned enough credits to qualify for benefits. If you became disabled right now your payment would be about............ $ 2,80l a month

*Family   If you get retirement or disability benefits, your spouse and children also may qualify for benefits.

*Survivors   You have earned enough credits for your family to receive survivors benefits. If you die this year, certain members of your family may qualify for the following benefits:

Your child..$ 2,131 a month

Your spouse who is caring for your child........................$ 2,131 a month

Your spouse, if benefits start at full retirement age ....$ 2,842 a month

Total family benefits cannot be more than.......................$ 4,974 a month

Your spouse or minor child may be eligible for a special one-time death benefit of $255.

Medicare   You have enough credits to qualify for Medicare at age 65. Even if you do not retire at age 65, be sure to contact Social Security three months before your 65th birthday to enroll in Medicare.

* Your estimated benefits are based on current law. Congress has made changes to the law in the past and can do so at any time. The law governing benefit amounts may change because, by 2034, the payroll taxes collected will be enough to pay only about 79 percent of scheduled benefits.

The earliest you can turn on your income (in most cases) is 62, and each year you wait beyond that—up to age 70—you receive a raise in your monthly benefit. At age 62 the individual whose statement is in Figure 2.1 would begin a lifetime income of $2,000 per month (with some caveats and adjustments we'll discuss later). We say "estimated" because the report is not exact. It makes assumptions about future income based on current income. If this person waited until 67 (full retirement age in this case), they would receive about $2,908 every month. If they were patient enough to wait until age 70, they would max out at a monthly income of around $3,610.

Collecting Social Security

To start collecting benefits, you need to apply online, by phone, or in person. Don't expect to receive a check in the mail, though: all SSI payments are now made via direct deposit.

If you activate your income, and then change your mind **within one year**, you can **revoke your claim**. You will need to pay the money back, and then it's like you never made the claim in the first place. Note that you can only undo your claim once; you can't claim and revoke multiple times.

If you've been collecting benefits for **more than a year** and then change your mind, you can still **suspend your claim**, which means turning your income back off. That will allow your monthly income amount to increase for a while until you turn it back on.

••

Medicare Part B premiums deducted from SSI

Once you sign up for Medicare coverage—a subject we will cover in detail in Chapter 5—if you are receiving SSI, your Part B premiums will be deducted from your monthly check.

••

"When" for Singles

If you are single, the decision about when to activate your income is pretty straightforward. Each year that you delay from age 62 to age 66, your monthly income increases by about 7.4% (it varies from year to year but that's the average). Waiting from 66 to 70 gets you an increase of 8% per year.

To put that in perspective, that is essentially a 7%–8% government-guaranteed rate of return that you earn by delaying the start of your Social Security income benefit. In this day and age of low interest rates, you likely won't find a comparable (safe) return like that in the investment markets.

Consider the person represented by Figure 2.1 again. He or she has three options: $2,000 a month at age 62, $2,908 a month at age 67, or $3,610 a month at age 70. Of course, waiting for the higher amount means forgoing years' worth of income that one could otherwise receive. So does it make sense to wait, or not?

Let's crunch the numbers. Using the data in Figure 2.1, we know that this person would get $24,000/year (= 12 times $2,000) if they start collecting at age 62, about $12K more per year if they waited until age 67 (a total of $34,896), and nearly twice as much ($43,320/year) if they waited until age 70. Table 2.A shows the cumulative income for this person at key ages.

Table 2.A: Cumulative SS Benefits for an Individual

Total Benefits Collected			
Age	Start at 62	Start at 67 (FRA)	Start at age 70
62	$24,000	$0	$0
67	$144,000	$34,896	$0
70	$216,000	$139,584	$43,320
75	$336,000	$314,064	$259,920
80	$456,000	$488,544	$476.520
85	$576,000	$663,024	$693,120
90	$696,000	$837,504	$909,720

You can see from this table why Social Security activation boils down to a bet on life expectancy. The various payment rates are designed so that if you live to your actuarial life expectancy you end up with about the same amount of money no matter when you turn the income on. At age 80 in the table, the three figures are in the same ballpark (ranging from about $450K to $490K). So if this person happened to die at age 80, it wouldn't have made much difference when he or she started to collect their benefits. (Remember that we are focused on single life calculations at the moment—an added layer of complexity is involved when you consider spousal and survivor income.)

But now suppose this person died at age 70, well before the average life expectancy. He or she would have gotten over $200,000 in benefits if they started collecting at age 62 and much less or nothing if they waited until age 67 or 70, respectively, to start collecting. On the other hand, if they live to 90 or beyond, they are clearly best off if they wait until age 70 to start collecting benefits. So if you think you're going to live for a very long time, it might be a good idea to wait until age 66 or 70 to get a higher monthly income.

A word about life expectancy

Since life expectancy is so integral to the subject of when to activate Social Security, it might be worth looking at the concept in more detail. According to government actuarial tables,[3] the average life expectancy for men at birth is 76, while for women the number is nearly 81. Given the table above, which suggests a break-even point around 80 years old, that suggests turning on SSI early is a bad bet for a man and an OK bet for a woman.

However, what really matters is your life expectancy at the claiming age of 62, which is when most people make the decision about when to turn on their income. At age 62, a man has a life expectancy of 82, and a woman nearly 85. Given those numbers, the odds favor waiting. Moreover, as we'll discuss next, there are aspects of planning for couples that make waiting an even more compelling option.

Often, when to take Social Security income goes hand in hand with a decision about whether or not to keep working. In that case, it's a quality-of-life question on top of a bet about life expectancy. And, like so many other issues involving money, it means tradeoffs between now and the future. If you work longer and delay taking Social Security, you can end up with much more money as you get deeper into retirement. Plus, as we discussed in Chapter 1, working longer—in the right job—can provide a sense of purpose in addition to cash flow.

The ideal scenario might be to find a way to keep working into your late 60s *in a job you enjoy*, while delaying when you need to tap into your investments and your Social Security income. Waiting means your income will increase 7%–8% each year, which is a pretty compelling risk-free rate of return.

Social Security Planning for Couples

For married couples, decisions about when to start collecting Social Security are much more complex. You have to consider the relative ages and life expectancy of both people, different earning levels, and (with heterosexual couples) the fact that women tend to outlive men.

In our experience, many people do not understand how Social Security works for couples, especially the fact that when one spouse dies, the other has the option to *keep the higher of their two incomes* (more on that in a bit). This lack of understanding can lead to lousy outcomes (especially for widows who often end up with lower income than they could have received with better planning).

Because of the complexity involved, we recommend using software that helps show break-even points based on your specific situation. Financial planners can provide a Social Security analysis (for a separate fee or as part of their broader suite of services), and there are free and paid programs you can access online such as:

- Open Social Security—A free, open-source Social Security calculator. https://opensocialsecurity.com/

- AARP Social Security Benefits Calculator—provided free by AARP, http://www.aarp.org/work/social-security/social-security-benefits-calculator.html

- Maximize My Social Security—$40 for an annual license, https://maximizemysocialsecurity.com/

The quality of output from Social Security software varies, with some providing detailed analysis and some providing rough estimates. Google "Social Security calculator reviews" and you will find a number of articles on the subject. Pay attention to whether or not the calculator you use has been updated to reflect changes made to Social Security rules in 2015 (more on that in a bit).

The most in-depth level of analysis will require you to enter your actual earnings history. Alternately, most programs utilize the estimates provided on your Social Security statement. Of course, make sure that you are dealing with a trusted source before providing personal details of any kind. **No analysis should require you to provide your Social Security number.**

In a little while we will take a look at the output from a Social Security analyzer to see how these software programs can guide your decision making.

When figuring out when to activate income, married couples should consider what happens if one of them passes away sooner than the other. And gentlemen, by "one of them," we mean you: 97% of Social Security survivor benefits are paid to women.[4] On average, heterosexual men marry women who are younger than they are,[5] and, as reflected in the Social Security actuarial tables, women live longer than men. The husband is also more likely to be the higher earner. These gender factors are very meaningful when it comes to Social Security planning.

Times are changing. The term "married couple" no longer assumes a man and a women (Social Security rules are now the same for gay and straight couples). And the pay gap between men and women is narrowing, particularly among millennials. So the scenarios that are most common now might not be as common in the future. That doesn't really matter, though ... all you need to know when making your decision is what the numbers look like for your particular situation.

Spousal Benefits

A key concept for couples is the **spousal benefit**. Married people can choose between two types of income: one based on their own earnings, or one based on a percentage of their spouse's benefit. In some cases the best approach involves switching between the two at some point. The spousal benefit is important because it allows a spouse who either did not work or did not have high earnings to earn an income that is based upon the income of the higher earner. We once helped a client couple discover that the wife was entitled to a higher benefit than she had been receiving. In fact, she received a check totaling tens of thousands of dollars to make up for the mistake. This was an unusual case because the Social Security Administration found that the wife had never been notified of the option to take a spousal benefit. Normally if you fail to claim the optimal amount of income, you will not be compensated for the difference. (Note that so-called "deemed filing" rules, which will be explained in the next section, make failing to claim your maximum income less likely.)

With the spousal benefit, as with the regular benefit, if you wait until full retirement age, you get a higher income. However, there is no increase if you wait beyond full retirement age to take the spousal option.

The maximum spousal benefit is 50% of what the other spouse would receive at FRA. So let's say your benefit is $800 a month, but your spouse (at FRA) is to get $2,000. Instead of taking your $800, you could opt to take the spousal benefit of $1,000 (= 50% of $2,000). Some key points on this topic:

1) You can't elect the spousal benefit until the other person has activated their own income. That is, if your spouse is still working and not claiming Social Security, you cannot claim a spousal benefit.

2) If you elect to receive either your own benefit or the spousal benefit prior to reaching FRA, your monthly benefit is permanently reduced (as discussed earlier).

3) The monthly amount is determined based on whether the person electing the spousal benefit has reached FRA, not whether the other one has gotten there or not. Let's say for example a woman is electing a spousal benefit. The husband's benefit sets the level of available income. The max spousal benefit is 50% of the husband's benefit (at his FRA) . . . but the amount is reduced if the wife elects it prior to *her* FRA.

Is all of this information giving you a headache yet? Writing it gave us headaches. The good news is that you don't really need to understand every single aspect of this complicated subject to achieve a successful plan. So bear with us while we continue to outline the basics, then we will talk about ways to figure it all out.

Survivor Benefits

In addition to the spousal benefit, the **surviving spouse benefit** is a critical element when it comes to Social Security planning for couples. In short, if the higher-earning spouse passes away, the survivor's income steps up to the level that the deceased had been receiving.

This has huge implications for women in heterosexual relationships, especially if they are from the Baby Boom generation and earlier. Not only do they usually live longer than their husbands, but they also tend to have earned less during life. In many cases they were homemakers without any earned income. If the husband turns on his income early and reduces his benefit, the woman can be stuck with a lower level of income for a very long time when she inherits his income.

Because of this, the optimal Social Security strategy for married heterosexual couples tends to be for the wife to turn her income (or spousal benefit) on at 62 so that the couple begins receiving some income early, while the husband waits either until full retirement age or until 70, in order to optimize his income and thus optimize the wife's survivor income. (This same rule applies for any couple where the higher-earning spouse has a lower life expectancy based on age, health status, etc.)

It is important to understand that survivor income is based on two factors:

1. When the deceased spouse turned on their Social Security income

2. When the surviving spouse turns on the survivor benefit

A surviving spouse can take the benefit as early as age 60, but the monthly income is permanently reduced if taken any time prior to their FRA. So, if possible, it might be best for the survivor to keep on his or her own income until FRA, before switching to the survivor benefit. As with spousal benefits, there is no advantage for a survivor to wait beyond FRA.

What about divorced couples?

The rules concerning divorce are complex and are beyond the scope of our willingness to explain endless details. The short version is that if someone is married for at least 10 years, they can be eligible for spousal and survivor benefits based on the earnings of their ex. In fact, the rules for divorced couples are somewhat more flexible than those for married couples. We refer you to ssa.gov/planners/retire/divspouse.html for more information.

Lapsed or Lapsing SS Spousal Rules

Due to rule changes adopted in 2015, some planning options for married couples are no longer available, or are being phased out:

- The so-called **file and suspend** strategy that allowed one person to claim their spousal benefit while both delayed their personal benefits has been done away with.

- A similar strategy, called **filing a restricted application**, is still available but only if you were born on or before 1/1/1954. This involves spouse 1 activating their income while spouse 2 takes spousal income, even though the latter's own benefit would be higher. This allows spouse 2's own benefit to continue to increase for a number of years (max of age 70), at which point they switch from spousal benefit to their own benefit. If you don't make the 1954 birthday cutoff, once you elect to turn on income, you are deemed to have elected the highest level of benefit available to you (the so-called **deemed filing** rule).

Social Security Scenarios for Couples

Enough chitchat, let's look at some examples. Our firm uses a couple of different software packages to analyze Social Security claiming strategies. One program is called **Savvy Social Security Planning**, and we will check out some of its output now. We'll look at three scenarios with varying ages and income levels for the spouses. The software calculates three possible approaches for each scenario:

- **Maximum Benefit**: the approach that provides maximum combined benefits over time if the husband and wife both live to life expectancy

- **Earliest Benefit**: the amount of income if both activate at 62 years of age (the most common age of activation), and then both live to life expectancy

- **Hybrid Strategy**: one of them turns on early at age 62, while the other waits until a later date (at which point the one who turned on early can switch to a spousal benefit)

Spoiler alert: the hybrid strategy typically provides the best overall projected outcomes.

Scenario 1: Heterosexual spouses are of similar age and the husband earns more

This is one of the two most common situations (we will look at the other one next). The chart and graph in Figure 2.2 depict results under the three different claiming strategies outlined above. In this case, we assume both parts of the couple live to their life expectancies (her 85, him 82).

In light grey box (upper graph) and solid light grey line (lower graph) we see the strategy that maximizes long-term results. In this case, the wife activates her income at age 66, the husband at 70 (at which point the wife switches to the spousal benefit of 50% of his benefit). In medium grey box (upper chart) and thick-dashed grey (lower graph) we see what happens if the couple activate as early as possible, both at age 62. In the black box (upper graph) and black dotted line (lower graph) we see the hybrid strategy, where the wife turns on her Social Security at 62, and the husband waits until the max age of 70 (at which point she switches to the spousal benefit).

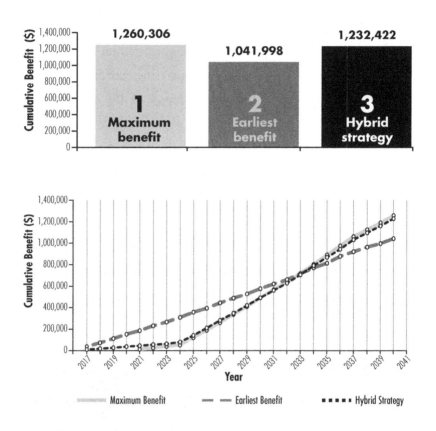

**Figure 2.2: Cumulative Benefit For Similar-Age
Couple with Higher-Earning Husband**

The Earliest Benefit scenario—both turning on at 62—is the most popular approach, and by looking at the graph you can see some appeal to it. For many years, the maximum outcome for the couple comes from activating early (we saw this illustrated by the data in Table 2.A for a single person). It's a tempting proposition: you can have a bunch of money coming in RIGHT NOW vs. you need to wait eight years (from ages 62 to 70), even though by waiting you might get more total benefit in the long run. And as you can see from the lower graph (dashed line), it does seem to work out well for a long time. For the equal-age couple

43

it maximizes total payments until they are 78 years old, at which point the more patient strategies begin to pull ahead.

So far, this sounds very similar to the single-person scenario we discussed earlier. But here's the key difference: remember, when one spouse dies, the income of the survivor may increase if the deceased spouse was receiving a higher income. And most of the time that means a higher-earning husband passing away and leaving a lower-earning widow.

Figure 2.3 shows the benefit received by a surviving wife (at the husband's life expectancy age of 82), and in that case the Earliest Benefit ("both turn on at 62") strategy has the worst results by far. In fact, **if the husband waits till age 70 to activate his income, the surviving wife will receive nearly twice as much income after his passing**.

Figure 2.3 Surviving Spouse Benefit for Equal-Age Heterosexual Couple

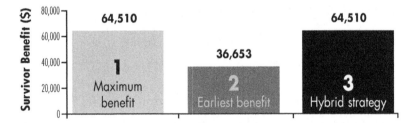

Hence the appeal of the hybrid strategy. If you take another look at the income graph in Figure 2.2, you'll note that the Hybrid Strategy line begins at the same time as the Earliest Benefit line (because the wife turns her income on right away in both cases), while the theoretical maximum long-term income approach—the light grey, Maximum Benefit, line—doesn't start until the wife is 66.

Couples should look at the Social Security claiming strategy with two goals in mind: maximize total income and maximize the outcome for the survivor. The hybrid strategy is a sensible approach that effectively straddles both goals.

Scenario 2: An older spouse has a higher income

Let's change the inputs a bit and see how the results differ. In this case, one spouse is significantly older than the other (gender is irrelevant). Figure 2.4 illustrates this common scenario where an older spouse has a higher income history. In this case it appears there are only two lines showing on the graph because the maximum long-term income strategy is the hybrid strategy, where the younger spouse turns on at 62 and the older spouse waits until 70—so the Maximum Benefit and Hybrid Strategy lines are identical. Don't worry if you just got confused, the concept is what counts, not the details. And we will summarize this all in a way that will hopefully provide clarity.

In this example the **crossover point** (see next page)—where the overall benefits favor waiting—is about age 78 for the older spouse and age 71 for the younger spouse.

Figure 2.4 Cumulative Benefit When Older Spouse Has Higher Income

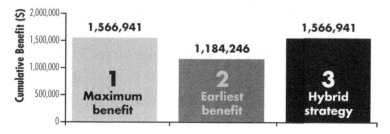

Figure 2.4 Cumulative Benefit When Older Spouse Has Higher Income (cont.)

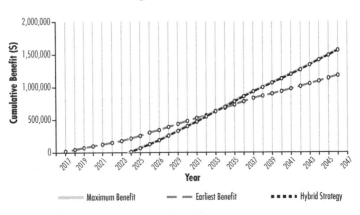

However, again the crossover point of total benefits is not the only variable to consider. The survivor income for the younger spouse is dramatically different if the older spouse holds off on activating their benefit until age 70 (Figure 2.5)

Figure 2.5: Survivor Benefits for Younger Spouse

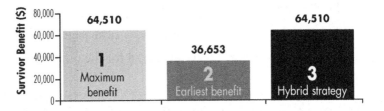

Scenario 3: Spouses are of similar age and earn similar money

A look at one more scenario reveals similar results. Figures 2.6 and 2.7 show that the hybrid approach has the husband activating at 62 while the wife waits until 70. No matter what ages or relative income levels we use, we get back variations on the same theme in terms of the outcome.

Figure 2.6: Cumulative Benefit when Spouses Are of Similar Age and Income

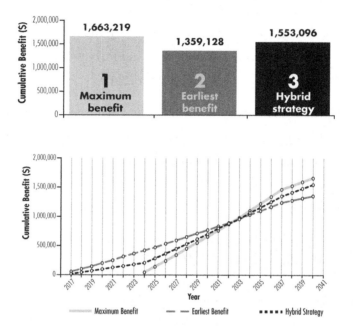

Figure 2.7: Survivor Benefit for Spouses of Similar Age/Income

Bottom Line for Married Couples

- Starting Social Security benefits at 62 for both spouses maximizes income for a period of time but results in a low income from a survivor perspective.

- Starting both incomes later (between full retirement age and age 70) maximizes results later in life, but it does take a long time for the crossover point to occur.

- The hybrid approach, where one person takes income early and the other waits until later, is typically the happy medium. **The couple gets the benefit of money coming in early on, but the survivor still receives a high survivor benefit.**

Taxation of Social Security Benefits

It might not surprise you to learn that the government, while giving you money, wants to take some of it back from you. Thankfully, most people receive their Social Security benefits tax-free. But depending on your overall level of income, some amount of your Social Security payments might be taxable. It's determined by a number called Modified Adjusted Gross Income.

Adjusted Gross Income (AGI) is calculated on your tax return, and includes investment income, capital gains, earned income, and so forth. For purposes of Social Security taxation calculation, you make the leap from AGI to Modified AGI by:

1) Adding back adjustments to gross income

2) Adding in any tax-exempt interest received

3) Adding ½ of the Social Security income received

Figure 2.8 shows various levels of Modified AGI—for single or married people—and what each means in terms of taxation of Social Security income (2018 data). For example, if you are a married couple earning more than $44,000 in Modified AGI, 85% of your Social Security income will be taxable.

Figure 2.8: Modified AGI Taxation

Married	Single	Amount Taxable
Less than $32,000	Less than $25,000	0%
$32,000-$44,000	$25,000-$34,000	50%
Over $44,000	Over $34,000	85%

On top of federal income taxes, some states take a piece as well. You can visit this site for a map showing which states tax SSI: http://www.kiplinger.com/tool/retirement/T055-S001-state-by-state-guide-to-taxes-on-retirees/index.php?map=tax-social-security#anchor

Is Social Security Going Broke?

Well, not quite yet. But trouble looms. Each year the government publishes an overview of the Social Security system's finances called the OASI Trustees Report. It runs almost 300 pages and is chock-full of data, so if you have trouble sleeping at night, we recommend you check it out: https://www.ssa.gov/OACT/TR/2017/. Actually, the summaries provided in the first 30 pages or so provide a pretty good sense of the problem we face.

Basically—and these estimates vary a bit from year to year based on actual claiming results and certain assumptions—the Social Security system is close to paying out each year more than it takes in that year. In fact, the 2018 OASI report suggests that this year payroll taxes taken in (plus interest earned on accumulated surpluses) will not be sufficient to cover benefits paid out. Previously, that wasn't expected to happen until 2022.

The government socked away reserves during the many years that it was taking in more than enough taxes to cover benefits, but those reserves are projected to run out in 2034. At that point, the system will be "broke." At least, from an accounting standpoint. There is no actual bank account holding a bunch of money earmarked for Social Security benefits. Rather, what we are talking about are various entries on government accounting ledgers. Moreover, there will always be payroll taxes coming in, just not enough to fully cover benefits, so the system wouldn't be completely insolvent. Nonetheless, from an accounting perspective the Social Security system is projected to be short of funding about 16 years from when we are writing this book.

The OASI Trustees Report makes projections looking 75 years out. According to the report, there are some fixes that could make the Social Security system stay solvent for that long. Either the annual payroll tax rate will need to increase by 2.76% (to 15.16%) on all workers, or benefits will have to be cut by 17% for current and future beneficiaries, or some combination of both.

Cutting benefits is a politically unpopular approach, to say the least. And Americans in or near retirement are a politically influential group (it's a large and growing population, and one that tends to vote more than younger people[6]). Plus, not many people like the idea of cutting the income of seniors. Given those factors—and the general tendency for nothing to get done in Washington these days—we think it is unlikely that benefits will be cut for those currently receiving them, or those approaching the initial eligibility age of 62.

On the other hand, it's fair to assume that a 2.75% payroll tax increase on all workers—the adjustment that would be necessary to balance the books—wouldn't be terribly popular either. So there is no easy way out of the problem.

But eventually, something is going to need to be done. The longer it takes to start fixing the financial imbalance, the greater the pain will be in terms of higher taxes and/or lower benefits. Some likely outcomes, in our opinion, are:

- delayed eligibility ages (particularly for those who have not yet reached 50 years old)

- increased taxation of benefits (particularly for high earners)

- removal of income caps for payroll taxes

Another possibility is a change in the way cost of living increases are calculated so that annual "raises" are not as high.

The bottom line is: something has to give. The problem highlights the need for people to have income plans for retirement—whether via working longer or from investments—that are beyond what is provided by Social Security.

Social Security Summary

More than two-thirds of Americans turn on Social Security prior to full retirement age, and the most common age is 62.[7] As we saw in the examples we reviewed, this early claiming approach has one glaring weakness: it can negatively impact the income of the surviving spouse. It also hinders long-term results if both spouses live to a ripe old age. We call this problem "early onset Social Security."

Given that a hybrid approach seems so broadly beneficial, why is early claiming so common? There is a mixture of factors at play.

According to a study by Voya, 60% of Americans end up retiring sooner than planned.[8] Some of those likely resulted from involuntary layoffs, some for health reasons. In any case, a lot of people experience retirement sooner than expected, and it makes sense that many of them are unprepared financially. A study by Experian says 71% of Americans feel they do not have enough saved for retirement.[9] Given the dearth of savings in America, even those who retire when they expect to aren't necessarily ready.

In other words, the primary reason why so many Americans turn on their income early is likely "desperation." People simply feel they have no other choice but to take as much as they can right away.

Another factor may be lack of knowledge or planning. A study by Northwestern Mutual suggests 35% of Americans have not spoken with anyone about retirement, and that includes their spouses![10] Only 27% have spoken with a financial advisor. This may be partly a "head in the sand" phenomenon. People who know they are in deep trouble in terms of their retirement savings may be choosing to ignore the issue altogether.

In any case, it is fair to assume that many Social Security recipients have never seen the kind of software analysis we looked at earlier, nor have they consulted with anyone knowledgeable about the pros and cons of various claiming strategies. Many may simply be unaware of the potential advantages of a hybrid claiming strategy.

Another problem is that while there is a wealth of information available on the internet about Social Security, it tends to come in the form of lots of rules and data, but not much actual advice. And the subject, as you have experienced while wading through this chapter, is complex and often confusing.

With that in mind, here are some practical steps to take to educate yourself and make smart decisions for you and your family:

- Visit ssa.gov and download your statement. Married couples should download statements for both spouses. Review them for accuracy.

- Analyze different claiming strategies based on your particular circumstances. A financial advisor can help, or you can do it yourself with the aid of software.

- Consider the results of your Social Security analysis in light of a full financial plan, which you can pursue via do-it-yourself services or with the help of a financial planner. We will revisit this in the last chapter when we talk about your overall action plan.

We recommend that you **schedule a visit to your local SSA office for a consultation**. You can find you local office by checking https:// secure.ssa.gov/ICON/main.jsp. Local help is available by phone or in person.

For in-person meetings, an appointment is not required but is highly recommended to avoid long wait times. The experience of our clients has been mixed when it comes to assistance in local SSA offices. The quality of help you will receive can vary from location to location. Some people rave about the helpful service they received, some rant about the lack of it. Almost anything that can be accomplished in person can also be done online, so if you are having a bad experience with the local people, try getting help online or via the main number: (800) 772-1213.

In short, as with the broader subjects of investing and financial planning, do not come at the subject uninformed. And do not be short-sighted about it. Future you will thank current you for giving serious consideration to what your needs might be many years down the road.

Endnotes

1   Social Security Keeps 22 Million Americans Out of Poverty: A State-By-State Analysis. https://www.cbpp.org/research/social-security/social-security-keeps-22-million-americans-out-of-poverty-a-state-by-state

2   Go to SSA.gov to find our more about maximum benefits.

3   Social Security Actuarial Life Table. https://www.ssa.gov/oact/STATS/table4c6.html

4   Policy Basics: Top Ten Facts About Social Security. https://www.cbpp.org/research/social-security/policy-basics-top-ten-facts-about-social-security

5   What's the Average Age Difference in a Couple? https://fivethirtyeight.com/features/whats-the-average-age-difference-in-a-couple/

6   Voter Turnout Demographics. http://www.electproject.org/home/voter-turn-out/demographics

7   When Should You Take Social Security? https://www.schwab.com/resource-center/insights/content/when-should-you-take-social-security

8   How to Plan for an Unexpected Early Retirement. http://corporate.voya.com/newsroom/media-highlights/how-plan-unexpected-early-retirement

9   Survey Results: Personal Finance. http://www.experian.com/blogs/ask-experian/survey-results-personal-finance/

10 2016 Planning & Progress Study. http://news.northwesternmutual.com/download/2016-planning-progress-financial-anxiety.pdf

CHAPTER 3

Five Money Maxims

In this chapter we are going to assume that you have some money saved for retirement, or at least you are beginning to save. Otherwise, you are going to have to figure out how to live on the income provided by Social Security (and perhaps pension income if you have that). Assuming you will have some retirement savings to manage, you will want avoid common pitfalls that can lead to poor investment returns and financial stress.

A company called Dalbar conducts an ongoing study estimating the investment returns of individuals, and the numbers are ugly. During the 30 years ended December 31, 2016, the S&P 500 averaged returns of 10.16%, while Dalbar estimates that stock mutual fund buyers only earned 3.98% per year[1] .

Why the disparity? Because human nature works against us. Our fear and greed instincts drive us into and out of investments at exactly the wrong times. When the market is falling and the headlines are scary, we want out. When things are going well and everyone is making money, we want in. That's the exact opposite of the recipe for success: buy low and sell high.

The problem is that the market does not act how we expect it to act. It surprises us, it moves counter to our intuitions. The best times to buy end up being when it seemingly makes zero sense to buy. At the height of the 2008 crisis, for example, there was not much going on that would have led a rational person to think "Things are looking up, this is a great time to buy stocks!" Remember, it was a truly scary time economically.

One of the things we commonly hear from investors when the market is correcting is, "I'm going to sell now and get back in when things calm down." Translation: "I'm going to sell now when the market is low, and buy back in later when it's higher."

TED Talk

Laurie Santos—A monkey economy as irrational as ours.

A scientist conducts economic experiments with monkeys seeking clues to why humans are often bad at investing

Thankfully there are some prudent steps you can take to avoid the mistakes that have led the average investor to poor results over the years. In this chapter we will look at five concepts—four related to investing and one related to spending—that we think form the basis of sound financial management.

Can Money Buy Happiness?

Studies suggest that money can buy happiness, at least to a point, although the effect may go away above a certain level of income. In fact, one study even provides a specific number, arguing that as income rises from zero up to $75,000, happiness rises with it.[2] But above that money has less of an impact. This makes some sense. The idea is that as you gain enough money to meet basic needs your emotional well-being improves, but after that it stops being a primary factor.[3]

Whether that's entirely true or not is debatable, and some data argues that the connection between wealth and happiness stays strong even as wealth goes up and up.[4] Also, there is research that suggests that how you spend your money is an important factor.[5] Hint: giving some of it away really helps!

···

We will look to investment history for important lessons, while describing the conditions that investors are dealing with today. In the next chapter, we'll talk about specific investment options. We'll also discuss whether you should get a financial advisor to help guide you, and if so, how to find a good one.

Our intent is not to provide a comprehensive guide to the world of investing. You would need to read multiple books to gain a broad understanding of the subject (you'll find some good examples on the library page of RetiredHappy.me).

So rather than taking a deep dive, we'll focus on five core concepts, while describing our own philosophy and preferred approaches.

1) Be patient: the stock market is not like Las Vegas

2) A moderate approach can help with challenging markets

3) Diversify your investments

4) Determine a safe level of spending

5) Understand current conditions

TED Talk

Michael Norton — How to buy happiness

Money may help you get happiness, if you use it the right way.

Maxim 1: Be Patient . . . The Stock Market Is Not Like Las Vegas

Have you ever stood too close to the TV and the picture is blurry, so you take a step back to see it clearly? That's how it is with investment markets. Below is a series of charts showing the movement of the Dow Jones Industrial Average over 1-month, 1-year, 10-year, and 100-year periods. Do you see how when you "step back" and take a longer view, the picture becomes clearer? (See Figure 3.1)

**Figure 3.1: Dow Jones Industrial Average (DJIA)
From Different Time Perspectives**

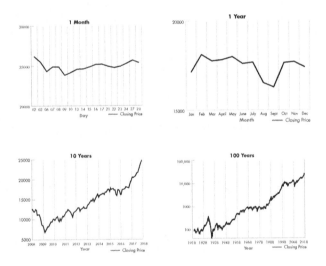

The stock market is often compared to Las Vegas. The comparison is apt in some ways. There are true stories (see books like *The Quants*[6] or *A Man for All Markets*[7]) about people who used techniques developed on blackjack and poker tables to make fortunes on Wall Street.

But the Las Vegas analogy is usually used to suggest that the stock market is risky, or is a bad bet for individual investors. As if, just as casinos are designed to fleece bettors, Wall Street is designed to rip off investors.

You can certainly lose big in the world of investments, whether by fraud (Bernie Madoff—see the referenced TED Talk) or calamity (the 2008 financial crisis). Wall Street can be a Bermuda Triangle for money. And the investment industry is constantly trying to invent new ways to lure fees and commissions out of the public. Sometimes with products and services that help investors, sometimes not.

TED Talk

Matt Weinstein — What Bernie Madoff couldn't steal from me

A man who lost his life savings in the Madoff fraud shares what he learned about what really matters in life.

But the stock market has been very good to those who approach it in a disciplined and patient manner. If you can employ Zen-like steadiness, time becomes your friend. It is actually a complete reversal of what happens in Vegas: **with the stock market, the longer you stay at the table, the more likely you are to win.**

Imagine if you walked into a casino and you could play a game where you bet on a dot that bounces up and down, and if the dot ends up higher than when you started the game, you won. But if it ends up lower, you lose. That's a decent analogy for stock investing. Look at the movement on the 1-month and 1-year charts shown earlier, that's Vegas: you don't know where you're going to end up. But look at the 10-year or 100-year charts. If you played our hypothetical "guess-the-dot game" and the movement of the dot over time was like the long-term market line, your odds of winning—of walking away with more money than you started with—would be great (assuming you were patient enough to wait for the dot to rise rather than quitting while it was low).

Market results support this concept. Let's consider the S&P 500 index from 1926 to 2010, a time frame that includes the Great Depression and the 2008 financial crisis. If you look at all of the one-year periods during that stretch, you will find that the index returned anywhere from +54% to -43%. Vegas, baby! But the variety of returns gets narrower as time frames get longer. In fact, if you owned stocks for any of the rolling 20-year periods from 1926 to 2010, the worst you could have done was an average annual return of 3%, and the best you could have done is 18%. That's not gambling, that's investing.

Figure 3.2: S&P 500 Index 1926-2010 (Overlapping returns annualized)

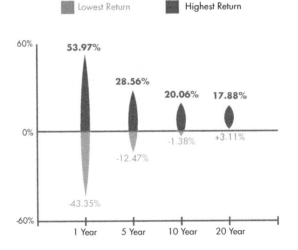

The market rise over a long period of time isn't because of magic, happenstance, or Wall Street chicanery. It rises because of human ingenuity. Again, consider the S&P 500. That index tracks the value of 500 of the largest public companies in America. In other words, some of the most successful businesses in the most successful economy in the world. The stock market's value represents hard work and innovation unleashed in a free capitalist society. Through economic calamities, World Wars, the Cold War, 9/11, and all manner of challenges, people continued to strive and innovate. Look around the world today and you will find plenty of reasons to fear, but you will also find businesses innovating like crazy. Our cellphones are practically supercomputers. There are cars that drive themselves. We may soon be able to say out loud, "I would like a pepperoni pizza," and it will arrive shortly via drone. It is easy to envision the worst, but humanity often surprises to the upside—and we find long evidence of that in the stock market.

When you make plans for your future based on expected investment performance, we suggest you keep your expectations on the low side of historical results. That said, regardless of market conditions, you should make use of the most powerful tool available to any investor: patience. The market is not a casino, it is a mechanism that allows you to participate in the growth of successful companies. Doing that successfully requires waiting through the ups and downs.

Maxim 2: A Moderate Approach Can Help With Challenging Markets

Yes, the market tends to go up if you wait long enough. But 20 years— the hold time that historically has always led to a positive result—is a long time. And it can be a rocky road along the way. So are there any other patterns you should be aware of that don't take so long to happen? Why, yes, yes, there are.

When we think about bad experiences in the market, we tend to think of big moves that happen over short periods of time, from a day to as long as a few years. The Great Crash of 1929 played out over two years. The crash of 1987 happened on one day. The impact of the 2008 financial crisis on the stock market, from the 2007 peak to the 2009 bottom, was 17 months. The 2010 Flash Crash lasted 36 minutes.

While the term **crash** is used to describe a fast downward move, the term **bear market** is used for drops that last longer. Sometimes there is overlap. What happened in 1929 to kick off the Great Depression could be described as both a crash and a bear market.

©Glasbergen / glasbergen.com

"For our next vacation, I'm taking the family to Wall Street.
They've got the most terrifying roller coaster I've ever been on!"

On the positive side, prolonged upward moves are described as **bull markets**. We don't seem to have a term to describe dramatic short-term rises in the market. Probably because there aren't any examples of the market rising 20% or more in a day.

With either bull or bear markets, there are two types: **cyclical** (short-term) and **secular** (long-term). When we look at market history, we see a series of secular bull and bear trends that lasted anywhere from 10 to 15 years.

In a **secular bull market**, we enjoy a nice long uptrend that mirrors the historical uptrend of the market. The most famous and impactful of those was the bull market between 1983 and 2000 (more on that influential period in a bit).

By contrast, a **secular bear** is a long stretch of time during which the market's movements are more random. In these periods stock prices may rise and fall quite a bit but ultimately the movement tends to be sideways. As seen below, we've been in a secular bear since the end of the Great Bull Market in 2000.

Figure 3.3: Secular (Long-term) Trend in S&P 500

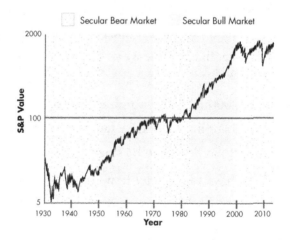

It is important to consider these secular cycles, because the strategies that work in one might not work in the other. Consider the Great Bull Market of 1983 to 2000. The modern financial industry developed during this period, because that's when mainstream America became widely involved with publicly traded stocks. The 401(k)

account, which became the dominant retirement savings vehicle and moved investment responsibility from the employer to the employee, was created in 1978. Stock mutual funds grew popular, and individual investors became stock buyers. Toward the end of this bull bonanza, day trading emerged, as the heady rise convinced many that the market could be used as a get-rich-quick scheme. (That ended badly, of course.)

During the Great Bull Market, the more stock you held in your portfolio, the higher your returns tended to be. The "risk tolerance questionnaire" became a key tool for helping people allocate money. The idea was that if you were young or you were comfortable with risk, you held more of your money in stocks, and you got a higher return. Or, if you were older or less risk tolerant, you held more money in bonds and you received a lower, steadier return.

This concept is still in wide use today. Here's the thing, though: in a secular bear market like the one we've been in since 2000, the "risk tolerance" approach doesn't work the same way it does in a bull market. For example, from 2000 to 2015, a retired investor drawing income from a 100% stock portfolio might have fared worse than one drawing from a balanced portfolio holding 60% stocks and 40% bonds.[8]

Moreover, you have to consider how the volatility of stocks will impact your behavior as an investor, and your stress level. The stock market dropped close to 40% in 2008, a breathtaking fall that chased a lot of people out of the market. If you were scared out toward the bottom of that correction, you may have missed the incredible recovery that started in 2009.

Someone in a balanced or "60/40" portfolio, on the other hand, would have been down about 22% in 2008.[9] That's still pretty scary, but not nearly as much as a 40% drop! A less dramatic drop isn't as likely to frighten an investor out of the market, and a smaller loss is easier to recover from when things turn around.

At the time of this writing, the market is near new highs, which might cause one to ponder if we are finally breaking out of a 17-year bear market into a new secular bull market. In which case, maybe we are back into a cycle where adding stock exposure will result in higher returns. Or maybe we are on the verge of another big correction that will continue the long sideways movement that began in 2000. We have no way of knowing how things will turn out—it will only be clear many years from now, when people can look back on what happened (which doesn't do us much good right now).

Prudence suggests that a moderate approach might make sense, especially for those in or near retirement. Once you no longer have income coming in from work, it becomes particularly important to safeguard the money that you have. There is a nearly infinite variety of asset allocations that you can employ (particularly when you factor in asset classes aside from stocks and bonds), but for simplicity's sake consider the following mixes of stocks and bonds that are commonly used to depict allocation options:

Stocks/Bonds

100/0—Aggressive

80/20—Growth

60/40—Growth & Income

40/60—Income & Growth

20/80—Income

0/100—Conservative

Generally speaking, the more stock you hold, the higher your expected level of return will be over the long run: a 100/0 or 80/20 mix is, in the long run, expected to have a much higher return than 20/80 or 0/100 mixes. (Though as we just discussed, that isn't always the case over shorter time frames, depending on market conditions.) But stocks are usually more volatile than bonds, so reaching for higher returns means accepting higher risk. The stock market periodically experiences double digit losses, which is far worse than the volatility typically seen in bonds.

When choosing your asset allocation, be sure to imagine what your reaction will be during the next big correction. Will you be scared out of the market (thus falling into a pattern of behavior that has historically hurt the returns of many investors), or will you be able to endure the ups and downs? If you are going to be overcome with fear during corrections, you might want to minimize your stock allocation (or maybe even avoid stocks entirely). Of course, with interest rates where they are, it can be hard to live on the income created by bonds alone.

For many in retirement a moderate allocation—somewhere between 60/40 and 40/60—seems to provide the right mix of risk and return. Using the Vanguard Balanced Index Fund as a proxy for the 60/40 portfolio, we found it lost about 22% in 2008, while providing a 10-year annual return (through the end of 2017) of 7%.[10] So ask yourself, could you stomach a drop of 22% (or perhaps worse) and be able to hang on?

It's important to have a serious discussion with yourself about risk. Think about your ability to handle having your investments significantly drop in value when the next correction comes (and it will come at some point). The time to prepare for bad markets is before they happen, by choosing an allocation that you can stick with through good times and bad.

Maxim 3: Diversify Your Investments

Don't put all your eggs in one basket, right? That's Investing 101, right up there with "buy low and sell high." But why? How does diversification impact you? Let's say you could spin a wheel and there would be one of five outcomes:

1) Win $10,000

2) Lose $2,000

3) Win $6,000

4) Stay even

5) Lose $4,000

Would you be willing to spin that wheel? Or would you rather spin a wheel with these options?

1) Win $5,000

2) Lose $1,000

3) Win $3,000

4) Stay even

5) Lose $2,000

The difference between these two win/lose scenarios represents how diversification is supposed to work. It provides a narrower range of expected outcomes. Let's say you put all your money in one stock, and that stock doubles in value. Boom, big win! But if the company goes out of business . . . boom, big loss! With diversification, the downside is that you give up the potential for the big win (just $5,000 instead of $10,000 in our example). But you reduce the potential for bigger losses as well.

Diversification works because you aren't actually playing just one game; you are spreading your bets among many games. Buying many different stocks lessens the possibility of a dramatic move in either direction.

It's a sound practice, and usually it works. Not only can you invest in 20 (or many more) stocks, but you can buy a variety of asset classes as well. For example, if you own stocks, bonds, international investments, commodities, and alternatives, each category should dance to its own tune. They all hopefully trend up over time, but their short-term gyrations are different. Because they move in different ways, you end up with a smoother overall experience than you would get by owning just one of them.

Unfortunately, when you need protection from volatility the most—during a crisis like '08—the panic can make everything move in the same downward direction. The fancy saying for that is: "All correlations go to one."

Another issue is that globalization has caused international economies to be more closely related, meaning that investing overseas doesn't provide as much diversification as it used to.

Diversification is not a perfect protection. But most of the time it does work. And it protects you from getting wiped out by a few bad bets.

Maxim 4: Identify a Safe Level of Spending

So you have been pretty smart and you've socked away a bunch of money for retirement. You're being patient. You've diversified. Then you retire and face the critical question: **How much of the stockpile can you safely spend each year without going broke?** Or, looked at a different way: while you are still saving, how much do you need to save to be able to create the income you need to support the lifestyle you want?

There is no exact right answer to this difficult question. But there are some rules of thumb, backed by academic study, that seem to make sense.[11],[12]

There are two schools of thought when it comes to spending retirement money. One is that you spend your money in a way that allows it to keep growing, so that the amount you are taking continues to grow at the level of inflation, and you leave behind an inheritance for your family, or charity, or both. The other is that you spend down your money so that you have a dollar or less left on the day that you die. The second approach is obviously hard to pull off exactly, but conceptually it means that you intend to spend more of what you have because you aren't terribly concerned about what you leave behind.

If you want to allow your money to keep growing, historical evidence suggests that you can safely spend about 4% to 4.5% of your money each year. So for example, if you have saved $1 million and have invested it in a balanced and diversified portfolio, you can take $40,000 per year (before taxes) out, and you should not run out of money. This assumes that you will hit some bad markets along the way, such as the tech wreck of 2000 and the 2008 financial crisis. Of course, there could be an even worse financial crisis looming that has not been accounted for in the data supporting the 4% rule. We have no way of predicting if that's the case or not.

The acceptable rate of withdrawal is much studied and much debated. While 4% to 4.5% is a common rule of thumb, some argue that higher levels can work and that the 4% rule causes people to be more frugal than necessary.[13] On the other hand, the data suggesting 4% as a safe rate is largely drawn from periods when bonds paid much more than they do now. Perhaps historically low interest rates mean that 4% may be too high a rate of withdrawal. With bonds paying less (and stocks expensive), it is reasonable to assume that the overall rate of return from investments going forward will be lower for a while, so the safe rate of withdrawal may be lower as well.

Not knowing what the future holds, our attitude is **to start with the 4% rule as a guide**, but be prepared to adjust depending on your individual needs and market conditions. The 4%—or whatever amount—that you pull from your investment portfolio will be added to whatever you receive from Social Security, and any pension income you might have, to form the basis of your retirement income.

One common way to access money from investments is to set up a monthly direct deposit from your investment account into your bank account. If you were reinvesting dividends and interest while saving for retirement, you might consider stopping the reinvestment during retirement. The dividends and interest can accumulate in a money market account, which will be used to feed the monthly transfer to your regular checking account.

Given today's low interest rate environment, it is unlikely that your overall portfolio will yield 4% (meaning pay dividends and interest that generate a combined 4% yield), so you will need to periodically sell some securities to keep replenishing the cash supply.

The Bucket Strategy

Some financial advisors advocate using a **bucket strategy** for accessing money from a portfolio. With this approach, you have your investments divided into short-, medium-, and long-term buckets. The short-term bucket holds cash and short-term bonds, and is drawn upon for income. The intermediate-term bucket holds bonds, and the long-term bucket holds stocks or other growth-oriented holdings. Periodically, as the short-term bucket is emptied you replenish it from the other buckets.

Some investors find clarity and comfort in the bucket approach, although it can be complicated to manage if you have a lot of different accounts. An alternative is to sell periodically from a variety of investments in a way that keeps you close to your targeted asset allocation. Ultimately, there probably isn't much difference either way, as the net result is the same: you are drawing from your investment portfolio in a measured fashion to support your spending needs.

What that spending looks like is up to you. Obviously, you need to meet your basic needs like housing, food, and healthcare. Beyond that is discretionary spending based on your priorities and desires . . . vacations, dining out, spoiling your grandchildren, or whatever else you want to spend money on. Make sure to track your spending and build a budget so that you can match your outflows to your available income in an effort to avoid financial stress (or ruin) later on.

....

Charitable giving

As part of your purposeful life, you may want to direct some of your money to charities. When supporting a charity, consider gifting appreciated stock instead of cash. In addition to a possible tax deduction for the gift, you avoid capital gains taxes on the appreciation (a tax-exempt charity can sell the stock and not pay any capital gains). Also, beyond age 70½ the IRS makes you take some money out of a traditional IRA each year whether you need it or not. If you don't need some or all of it and use that portion to make a gift directly to a charity from the IRA, you can avoid income taxes on the distribution. Talk to your IRA account provider for details.

....

Maxim 5: Understand Current Conditions

It has often been said that the four most dangerous words in investing are "This time is different."

A financial crisis is typically preceded by a sort of mass delusion. People begin to believe that the time they live in is unique. They ignore fundamental risks such as too much debt or overvalued assets. In a bubble, people are making big money, and everyone wants in.

A notable example is the tech wreck of 2000–2002. Investors came to believe that in the dotcom era the rules of business had changed, and valuations no longer had to be based on something as "trivial" as earnings. This partly resulted from people being astonished by how amazing and cool the internet was. Likewise, in 1637, at the height of the Tulip Mania, the populace was blown away by a fancy flower.

So it is with some trepidation that we say: this time *is* different.

In September of 1981 the rate on the 30-year Treasury bond hit a peak of 15.08%. Can you imagine earning a risk-free rate of return that high? Seems like a dream come true in light of today's low interest rates (the 30-year hit an all-time low of 2.11% in July of 2016).

Figure 3.4: U.S. 30-Year Bond Yield

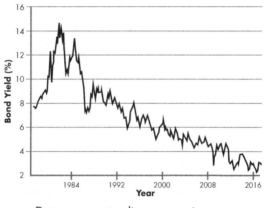

Data source: tradingeconomics.com

Of course, rates were high back in the '70s and '80s for a very bad reason: inflation. Inflation is the invisible killer of money. Each year (except in rare periods of deflation, another sort of problem) inflation eats away at the buying power of your savings. It acts as a relentless negative rate of return that hurts your ability to save for the future.

In 1979 inflation exceeded 13%. That's a serious loss of value, and that's why interest rates were so high. Bond buyers demanded a high rate of interest to offset the inflation.

Since that time, interest rates have, with minor interruptions, spent decades in a state of decline. They eventually approached zero as the Federal Reserve and other central banks used low rates to resurrect the global economy in the wake of the 2008 crisis.

So, *this time*—the second decade of the 21st century—is different in the sense that we can't really compare it to any other period. But what's as true today as it has ever been is that we do not know what the future holds. Things will change. Presumably, interest rates will move higher in the years ahead. Even if they don't go higher, we know they can't go much lower.

One concern with the current environment is that bonds lose value when interest rates rise. Let's say you buy a bond that pays 4%, and interest rates rise so that new bonds with a similar maturity pay 5%. No one is going to buy your lousy 4% bond when they can buy a shiny new bond at 5%, unless you sell it for less than you paid for it. If you hold your bond until maturity, it will still pay off at full value, but during the intervening time it will show as a loss of value in your portfolio.

The other problem with low rates is simple: bonds that you can buy now don't pay much. It used to be common for retirees to get a significant portion of their retirement income from very safe investments like FDIC-insured Certificates of Deposit (CDs). Nowadays, one-year CDs typically pay closer to 1% (again, that's a figure that may be different by the time you are reading this). To put that in perspective, at 1% you would need $5 million just to create an income of $50,000. And that's before taxes.

If rates rise in an unexpectedly fast fashion, it could hurt stock and bond prices. We do not know if that will happen, but we do know that the bonds we buy today have very low rates. And we also know that stock prices are expensive compared to most other times in history.[14] Our belief based on those facts is that investors should temper their expectations for returns in the coming years.

Financial planning, a topic we will revisit in Chapter 10: The Retirement Happiness Map, involves gathering information and making projections about the future. But because there are so many variables involved, the projections aren't likely to be very accurate beyond a few years out. So what you are really doing when planning is determining whether you appear to be pointed in the right direction at any given time. For that you need to rely on tried-and-true principles, along with an understanding of current conditions. For example, the 4% "safe" withdrawal rate is tried and true, but currently we are dealing with very low interest rates and expensive stocks, factors that should be taken into account.

Change is constant. Your personal situation will change, you will pass through different stages of life, and the economy and the markets will experience varying conditions. Because of that it is important to think of financial and investment planning as an ongoing process. You should take the time to update your financial plan periodically—every few years or annually as you move through periods of transition such as when you approach and enter into retirement.

Our Financial Advice in a Nutshell

If we had to boil financial planning and investment management down to one sentence, it would be this: split your investments into a well-diversified mix of stocks, bonds, and other holdings; think long-term even when things get scary; take out about 4% per year (or less) from your investments each year; and update your financial plan periodically to make sure you are pointed in the right direction. That's a simplification, of course, and circumstances may dictate variation, but essentially that is what we believe in.

Always bear in mind that the future cannot be foretold. Ignoring that truth and attempting to know what can't be known is a recipe for stress and lousy investment results. Consider a bit of wisdom called the Serenity Prayer:

> *God grant me the serenity to accept the things I cannot change,*
>
> *Courage to change the things I can,*
>
> *And wisdom to know the difference.*

There are elements of this prayer that apply to investing. You need enough wisdom to recognize what you cannot know and change about the markets, you need courage to take charge of your financial situation and face investment risk, and you need serenity to get through the difficult times.

Endnotes

1   The Dalbar Study: 30 Years of Average Equity Fund Investor vs. Indexes. https://www.ifa.com/articles/dalbar_2016_qaib_investors_still_their_worst_enemy/

2   Happiness, Income Satiation, and Turning Points Around the World. https://www.nature.com/articles/s41562-017-0277-0

3   High Income Improves Evaluation of Life but Not Emotional Well-being. http://www.pnas.org/content/107/38/16489

4   Economic Growth and Subjective Well-Being: Reassessing the Easterlin Paradox. http://users.nber.org/~jwolfers/papers/EasterlinParadox.pdf

5   Presocial Spending and Happiness: Using Money to Benefit Others Pays Off. https://dash.harvard.edu/handle/1/11189976

6   *The Quants: How a New Breed of Math Whizzes Conquered Wall Street and Nearly Destroyed It* by Scott Patterson. ISBN-13: 978-0307453389

7   *A Man for All Markets: From Las Vegas to Wall Street, How I Beat the Dealer and the Market* by Edward O. Thorp. ISBN-13: 978-0812979909

8   Why a 100% Stock Portfolio Can Ruin Your Retirement. https://www.marketwatch.com/story/why-a-100-stock-portfolio-can-ruin-your-retirement-2016-03-22

9   Vanguard Balanced Index Fund Performance. https://advisors.vanguard.com/VGApp/iip/site/advisor/investments/performance?fundId=0002

10   Vanguard Balanced Index Fund Annual Report. https://www.vanguard.com/funds/reports/q020.pdf

11   Portfolio Success Rates: Where to Draw the Line. https://www.onefpa.org/journal/Pages/Portfolio%20Success%20Rates%20Where%20to%20Draw%20the%20Line.aspx

12   Sustainable Withdrawal Rates From Your Retirement Portfolio. http://afcpe.org/assets/pdf/vol1014.pdf

13   Breaking the 4% Rule. https://am.jpmorgan.com/blob-gim/1383280103367/83456/RI-DYNAMIC.pdf?segment=AMERICAS_US_ADV&locale=en_US

14   Goldman Warns That Market Valuations Are at Their Highest Since 1900. https://www.bloomberg.com/news/articles/2017-11-29/goldman-warns-highest-valuations-since-1900-mean-pain-is-coming

CHAPTER 4

Managing Your Nest Egg

What if we were to describe the secret to the investment universe, the one perfect strategy that leads to consistent profit and a life free from financial worry? That would be awesome! But as best we can tell, and we have spent a fair time looking for it, there is no such thing.

The investment markets are infinitely complex. Even the Wall Street pros—equipped with Ivy League educations, sophisticated systems, ample capital, even inside information—often find themselves humbled by the market.

That's the bad news. The good news is that investing can be simplified, and that simplification often improves results.

In this chapter, we'll talk about the pros and cons of some popular investment approaches. Our goal is to boil investing down into some fundamental principles that, when consistently followed, tend to provide good results.

First we will discuss different kinds of accounts you can hold your investments in—because that can make a big difference when it comes to taxes—and then we'll talk about common investment options and how they might fit into your personal strategy. Finally, we'll talk about the different types of advisors that are available if you want to get some help.

We caution that this is not meant to be a comprehensive guide to investing, but rather a strategic overview. To manage your finances and investments successfully, you'll need to take a deeper dive into the subject, whether with or without the assistance of an advisor.

What Are You Going to Invest In?

Asset allocation, as we discussed in the previous chapter, means deciding how much of your money to put in different categories. That could include stocks, bonds, commodities, real estate, and various alternatives (more on that subject in a bit). How to allocate should be your first investment decision, because it will largely determine how quickly your money will grow, and how much risk you will have to put up with. Many investors agonize over which individual stocks to buy—a choice that might be better determined with a coin flip—when devoting more thought to how much to put into various asset categories would probably have a far bigger impact on returns.

Here's why: In a diversified portfolio of stocks, the performance of any one of them won't make or break you. But the decision to buy all stocks, or all bonds, or a mixture of both (and perhaps other categories) will make a huge difference—in the short run because the mix you choose will decide your risk and volatility, and in the long run because it will determine your returns.

Figure 4.1: Factors that Impact Portfolio Performance

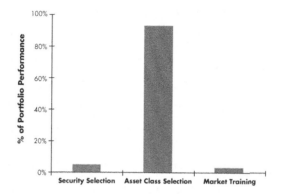

Financial Analysts Journal, July/August 1986. Data source: CEG Worldwide/Gary P. Brinson, L. Randolph Hood, and Gilbert L. Beebower

Stocks and Bonds

Let's have a quick refresher on stocks and bonds.

When you buy a stock, you are buying a piece of the company. Buy one share of Microsoft and you just became a part owner of Microsoft. Pretty cool, right? And if you buy shares in an S&P 500 Index fund (more on index funds later), you become a part owner of 500 of the biggest public companies in the U.S. Stock investing has historically provided strong returns because America has a lot of great companies that have created tremendous value over time. And while some companies fail or struggle, on the whole American companies (and for that matter many international companies) have been good things to own a piece of.

Of course companies, and economies, go through ups and downs. The value of individual businesses, and of businesses as a group, can rise and fall rapidly at times. And with them the value of stock owned by investors. These movements in value are unpredictable. Stock owners become stressed and fearful when their investments lose value, which can lead to bad investment decisions. So stocks offer the potential for strong long-term returns, at the cost of high short-term risk.

Bonds are a more predictable option. A bond represents debt. The company (or government entity) is borrowing money from people who buy their bonds. The bond holder gets paid interest, and at maturity they get the amount they "loaned" back. It's fairly predictable, but the rate of interest is usually well below what stockholders earn over time. We'll talk about bonds again later, but for now just understand the critical relationship illustrated by stocks and bonds: higher risk equals higher return, and vice versa. It is a rule nearly as immutable as gravity. And much like gravity, you ignore it at your peril.

Which to choose? The decisions are not easy. This seems like a difficult time to be an investor. Stocks, by most traditional metrics, are expensive. Maybe that will have changed by the time you are reading this (hopefully not in too dramatic a fashion!), but that is the reality as of the time of this writing. In fact, the only time they were more expensive was prior to the "tech wreck" correction of 2000-2002.

With stocks expensive, should we avoid them entirely? Maybe not. History shows that high valuations don't necessarily predict a correction. Former Federal Reserve Chairman Alan Greenspan famously described "irrational exuberance" in the market in 1996, nearly four years before the tech wreck correction arrived. An expensive market can continue to appreciate, and missing out on those gains can hurt your long-term investment results.

While an expensive market is not predictive of a correction, it does suggest below-average returns in coming years.[1] While we can't say with any great confidence that a correction is about to happen, it is certainly possible. Moreover, it is reasonable to fear that returns will be subpar for a while.

As we have already described, the bond market is no picnic either. Aside from sitting on cash—and losing value to inflation—what else is there? That brings us to the broad category of "alternatives."

Alternative Investments: Not stocks, not bonds

Alternative investments (**alts**) is a term that encompasses everything that is not stocks and not bonds. This is a very broad subject, but examples include:

> **Commodities**—Hard assets such as oil, gas, agricultural products and precious metals. Because commodities tend to be economically sensitive, they can sometimes be highly correlated to stocks.

> **Managed futures**—A "future" or **futures contract** is an agreement to buy or sell a certain quantity of a commodity at a specified time and price. Managed futures portfolios are investment vehicles that actively trade these contracts. There are commodity, currency, interest rate, and stock futures. You can choose from a number of managed futures mutual funds (or private placements, but those have high minimums and

can be illiquid). Managed futures provide low correlation to stocks and bonds, and they are one of the few asset classes that did well during the 2008 meltdown.[2] Like stocks, though, the category has its ups and downs.

Hedge funds—A broad category of investment vehicles that are typically available only to high-net-worth investors. Hedge funds were originally intended to "hedge" or reduce risk in a portfolio, but these days some are highly leveraged and risky. Hedge funds have come under fire in recent years for high fees and subpar performance, although some of them still live up to the original goal of reducing portfolio risk.

Venture capital (VC)—Another category that is mostly available only to high-net-worth investors, VC involves investing in very early stage businesses, in hopes of latching onto the next Google or Amazon. It's a category with extremely high risk but also with the potential for extremely high returns (or losses).

Private equity—Similar to venture capital, but private equity involves buying companies that are more mature, with the idea of improving the business and selling it later at a profit. This category may provide better returns than stocks, but your money is locked up for as long as 10 years. And again, it's not usually available to investors of average means.

Real estate—The most common way to hold real estate is as a homeowner. Some people downsize their home in retirement as a way of "cashing out" of their real estate. You can also invest in Real Estate Investment Trusts ("REITs") that trade like stocks. Some investors purchase rental properties (residential or commercial), or participate in partnerships. Real estate can be a good diversifier, although since it is economically sensitive, it can also move in the same direction as stocks—the 2008 crisis being the most notable example of that.

Lottery tickets—Just kidding, but more on this in a bit.

The theoretical ideal with alternatives is something that provides a return as good as the stock market, with but with a different kind of volatility.

Imagine if you could own an investment that provided the same long-term return as stocks, but the short-term moves were exactly opposite those of the market. In other words, when stocks rise, the other investment falls, and vice versa. That's called inverse correlation, and on a chart it would look like Figure 4.2:

Figure 4.2: Opposite-Behaving Investments

If you could find such a thing, your portfolio would enjoy no volatility but high returns, as indicated by the straight line rising in the figure. Surely this would be the holy grail of investing.

In reality, there are no perfectly inversely correlated investments that trend higher over time. Lacking the perfection of inverse correlation, what we seek in alternatives is non-correlation. In other words, investments whose movements are minimally related to those of stocks. Low correlation means that when the stock market falls, the alternative investment may or may not fall at the same time.

It's fairly easy to find investments that have low correlation to stocks, but the trick is finding ones that have low correlation and positive returns over time. It doesn't do you much good to diversify into an asset class with flat or negative returns. Lottery tickets, for example, provide non-correlation to stocks, but usually they're a terrible investment.

Finding good alternatives has been challenging in recent years, as some trading strategies—such as those employed by many hedge funds—have struggled in the wake of the 2008 crisis. One theory is that intervention by central bankers around the world changed conditions in the markets, interfering with trading tactics that used to work well. If that's the case, perhaps as central bankers pull back from their interventions, alts will do better. Another theory is that there are too many different funds trying to use the same strategies, such that competition reduces the profit potential. If that's the case, the problem might persist into the future.

An argument can be made for keeping your portfolio and investment mix simple, and just sticking to stocks and bonds. That's not the approach we take, especially given pricey stocks and low interest rates. But if you want to manage your own portfolio, the complexity presented by alternative investments might not be worth the trouble.

Mutual Funds: To index or not to index

Mutual funds are a common and easy way to invest. They allow you to purchase a bunch of investments—stocks, bonds, or whatever else—all at once. Mutual funds can help achieve one of the money maxims we talked about in the previous chapter: diversification.

A hot topic these days is the use of **index mutual funds.** An index is a collection of stocks (or other investments) used to track the market or some part of it. The S&P 500 Index, for example, is made up of 500 of the largest publicly owned companies in the U.S. The Dow Jones Industrial Average is another well-known example. The Dow is 30 stocks from different industries meant to provide a representation of the overall economy. There are indexes that track different sizes of companies. Some track companies in certain countries or industries. And there are indexes for various asset classes (bonds, real estate, commodities, and so forth).

In a traditional mutual fund, as opposed to an index fund, there is a manager or team of managers who are paid to decide which stocks or bonds to purchase for the fund. The manager receives a fee for this service, and hopefully their expertise leads to good results.

The mutual fund world can be further broken down into **loaded** or **no-load** funds. Loaded funds include an additional fee (load) that compensates an investment advisor who recommends the fund to investors. No-load funds do not carry this additional fee. In recent years, as advisors have become more likely to be compensated by asset management fees, loaded funds have become less common.

Unfortunately, the majority of managed funds have failed to beat their target indexes.[3] So, for example, most managers who are picking large companies for their Large Cap fund have not beaten the S&P 500 Index. That's where index funds come in. They simply invest in the stocks that make up the index, and since they require no manager, they have very low costs of operation.

The average managed stock mutual fund has annual expenses of 0.82%, while the average stock index fund has expenses of .09%, and some are even less expensive than that.[4] Mutual fund fees (and asset management fees) come directly out of the value of your investments, and they can add up over time. **A $10,000 investment earning 10% for 10 years is worth $25,937.** If we reduce the rate of return to 9.27% to represent the average difference in fees between managed funds and index funds, the result is only $25,308, a difference of $629. That gap will be more dramatic as the time frame and dollars invested get larger.

Now, if a manager is really good and outperforms the index, the results can skew in the other direction. But as we said, most managers do not beat their indexes. Plus it is hard—some argue impossible—to predict which managers are going to be among the few that beat their index.

This reality has led to a movement toward the use of index funds by individual and institutional investors.

We do not argue with the wisdom of indexing. But in our own practice, for a variety of reasons, we use a mixture of index funds and managed funds. First, we think the advantage of index funds is overstated a bit by focusing on how the "average" fund performs against the index. The biggest advantage that index funds enjoy is lower fees. So if you eliminate funds with above-average fees, you may change the odds of choosing a manager who will match or exceed the results of the index. Note that even the most iconic company in the index-fund world—Vanguard—also offers a suite of (low-cost) managed funds. Also, volatility needs to be considered in addition to performance. If a manager is obtaining good performance with lower-than-average risk, they are providing a different sort of value.

We also have a philosophical concern about index funds. If, to consider a theoretical extreme, everyone invested only in indexes, there would no longer be a market. The market is a pricing mechanism that assigns value based on business success and failure. Businesses that are doing well should be assigned a higher value than businesses that are not. Indexing removes that pricing mechanism. All businesses are bought and sold simply by virtue of being in the index. If indexing continues to gain popularity, stocks that are in the index will gain an artificial valuation advantage over stocks that are not. Perhaps that argues further for owning the index, but perhaps it represents a bubble of sorts, something that will end badly.

We don't pretend to be able to foresee how that issue might play out. But being in the habit of spreading our bets, we find some comfort in owning a mixture of indexes and managed funds. Even acknowledging the drag that investment fees cause on returns, **we like to use managed funds (typically with below-average expenses), alongside index funds**.

The firm we work for has an entire team dedicated to picking mutual funds based on performance and volatility history, investment strategy, expenses and so forth. And yet we still see the value of indexing and include it in our portfolios. For the individual investor who lacks the time or inclination to research funds, indexing is a good way to go.

In fact, the numbers suggest you will maximize your results with that approach.

. . . .

Target-date mutual funds can target the wrong date

Like index funds, target date funds have exploded in popularity. And like index funds, we think they are largely beneficial, but we have some misgivings about them.

First, the good. Above all, target date funds are easy. Planning to retire in 2025? Buy the XYZ (they are offered by many fund companies) 2025 Fund. The idea is that they start you out with a high percentage of your money in stocks, and over time the portfolio becomes less and less aggressive until at retirement you are mostly invested in bonds.

It makes some sense, and the simplicity seems to encourage people to invest when they might otherwise be put off by the headache of building a portfolio. They have become very popular inside 401(k)s.

The problem is that with interest rates as low as they are, can you really afford to retire with most of your money in bonds? Target-date funds seem to be tailor-made for the investment conditions of the '80s and '90s, when interest rates were much higher. But now, with rates low and potentially rising, an investment that leaves you with 70% or so of your money in bonds could be a recipe for trouble. At age 65 the average life expectancy is about 20 years. That's a long time to make your money last, and it might be hard to do with the bulk of your assets in low-yielding bonds. Plus there is the risk of bonds losing value as interest rates rise.

If you want something simple, a balanced fund that splits money between stocks and bonds (perhaps with a ratio somewhere between 40/60 and 60/40) might be a better choice than a target-date fund.

. . . .

Annuities — The Good, the Bad, and the Ugly

Annuities are insurance-based investments. They are designed to offer a guarantee. It could be a guaranteed stream of income, or a promise that you won't lose money, or that your heirs will receive an inheritance.

There are many different kinds of annuities, and explaining them all is beyond the scope of this book. Besides, writing a lot about something so boring is beyond the scope of our patience.

But we do think it is important to address the pros and cons of two of the most popular forms of annuities: variable and indexed.

Variable Annuities

The most popular form of these products is the variable annuity (VA). The easiest way to think about a VA is like a bunch of mutual funds with some sort of insurance wrapped around it. It's more complex than that—in fact, complexity is one of our biggest concerns when it comes to annuities—but that's the basic idea. You choose from a menu of investment options within the annuity (sort of like within a 401(k) or other retirement plan), and hopefully it grows for a period of years. With most VAs the idea is to eventually activate an income stream for retirement. As with retirement plans, annuities can provide tax deferral on investment gains, and there can be tax penalties for pulling money out prior to age 59½.

Variable annuities come with a variety of different features and benefits, and each insurance company sells its own versions of them, with different nuances. This all adds to the mind-bending complexity of the products.

Most variable annuity policies come with a minimum **death benefit** (how's that for an oxymoron!) that assures that *even if the investments drop in value*, your heirs will receive back at least the amount you invested (minus any withdrawals you might have taken).

The other common form of annuity insurance is called a **living benefit**. A living benefit guarantees you will receive a stream of income for a period of time, typically for the rest of your life.

The most popular sort of living benefit these days is the Guaranteed Minimum Income Benefit (GMIB), where the annuity company promises you a certain level of income regardless of the actual performance of the annuity. The money inside the annuity is invested in a diversified portfolio of **separate accounts**, which are basically mutual funds. The value of the accounts rises and falls depending on how the money is invested and what is happening in the markets. At some point, you activate the income from the annuity and start receiving a monthly check. For example, let's say you invested $200,000 with a guaranteed 5% benefit, and you let it grow for a while. If 10 years later the annuity was valued at $400,000, you could begin to take an income of $20,000 per year (5% of $400,000), or $1,667 per month. With a GMIB, the insurance company will guarantee that you (and possibly your spouse) will receive that $20,000 annually for life, no matter what happens to the value of the contract in the future.

Drawbacks and Concerns

Here's the thing, though: when you first start drawing income from a variable annuity you aren't really getting money from the insurance company, you are just pulling out the money you put in (plus any investment gains). And on top of that, the insurance company is taking out fees, which often add up to 3%–4% annually (that includes fees associated with the underlying investment funds, fees to compensate the advisor, and fees for the insurance coverage).

In theory, if the market is doing well, the contract can continue to grow in value even after you start drawing income from it—a possibility we feel is sometimes used to exaggerate the benefit of these products. But in reality, **the withdrawals and the fees present a high hurdle**, and there is a good chance that your annuity will decline in value over time once you start to take income from it.

Another concern we have already referenced is that the VA contracts are complex and people often struggle to understand the features, benefits, and drawbacks of the product. We know of at least one variable annuity that comes with a **disclosure document** that is literally the size of a phone book (we assume that the audience for this book is old enough to remember what a phone book is).

In our opinion, there is an unholy union between our political system and our legal system that has led to investors being buried by long, confusing disclosure documents. In theory these documents are meant to inform and protect investors. In reality they mostly seem designed to provide legal cover to companies selling investment products. Much of the endless legalese is mandated by law. We are experienced investment professionals and find some disclosure documents almost unreadable! What hope does the average investor have of understanding them?

We fear that many who invest in variable annuities don't entirely understand what they are buying. In some cases this allows unscrupulous advisors or insurance sales people to take advantage by exaggerating the benefits annuities provide, or by failing to explain the costs and risks that are involved.

Another problem with variable annuities is that they typically lock you in with back-end fees. When you invest you sign a contract, and the contract typically says that if you change your mind and ask for your money back, you will pay a penalty fee (except within the 30-day legally mandated look-back period). A back-end fee of 7%–9%—which declines to zero over a period of years—is typical.

On The Other Hand ...

Expensive, confusing, illiquid . . . why would anyone ever buy a VA? Despite these drawbacks, there are times when variable annuities prove to be good investments.

Let's say you are retired and you are taking 5% out of a traditional portfolio (not an annuity) every year, and suddenly the economy enters a prolonged fall. You are watching your nest egg disappear over time as you pull out money to support yourself, and it seems like the market will never stop falling.

What do you do? Can you just sit still while your money evaporates? This is when the annuity can become attractive. Even if the market stays bad for a long time, and you draw your contract down to zero, the annuity company has to keep paying you income for life. (Or, depending on how it was set up, for your life and the life of your spouse.)

In reality, this rarely happens, otherwise insurance companies wouldn't stay in business. However, despite all the criticisms about VAs being overpriced, the 2008 crisis revealed that many insurance companies had actually been over-generous with their guarantees. Crashing markets meant that insurance companies lost money as investors benefited from the protections built into their policies. In the wake of the crisis, some investors will receive income payments for life despite having drawn annuity policies down to zero, because of the living benefits built into their policies.

An aspect of all this that is hard to quantify is the peace of mind VAs can provide in bad markets. Imagine if you retired somewhere near October 9, 2007 (the peak of the market just before the global financial crisis began). In the months that followed, you would have watched your life savings dwindle away. What would you do? As we have discussed, it's typically a bad idea to sell during corrections. But with headlines shouting doom and gloom, and the market dropping on almost a daily basis, would you just hold on for dear life and hope for the best?

If a portion of your investment portfolio was insured, maybe you would. Maybe having some money in a vehicle that provides a stream of income for life would give you the confidence to hold still and ride out the financial storm.

It might be said that annuities are poor investments in rising markets, but good investments in plunging markets. A mathematical argument can be made that annuities should always be avoided, but when you factor in the peace of mind they are able to provide in scary times, we think they are worth consideration.

Not every aspect of investing can be described with numbers. Human beings are involved. Fear can be a big factor when it comes to

investing, and should be taken into account when putting a portfolio together.

Finally, in a time of low interest rates, annuities are a way to create a reliable stream of income. In that sense they should be compared to bonds to determine if they fit into the mix as a fixed-income investment. In fact, when you factor in the fees, they may end up performing more like bonds than stocks over time.

Bottom line: If you are going to put some of your money in a variable annuity, you need to understand the drawbacks as well as the potential benefits. Unfortunately, that may involve wading through a phonebook-sized disclosure document. If someone tries to sell you a variable annuity without describing the downsides—cost, complexity, and illiquidity—you might want to consider running away from that person.

Fixed Indexed Annuities

Another form of annuity that has become quite popular in recent years is the **fixed indexed annuity**. As with variable annuities, we see potential value but fear the product is sometimes misrepresented to investors. Thankfully, they are a bit less complex than VAs.

While a variable annuity could be described as a portfolio of mutual funds with insurance wrapped around it, an index annuity is somewhat less complex. You make an investment, receive some interest over a period of time, and then you get your money back. With an index annuity, the rate of interest will be determined based on the performance of a certain index (for example, the S&P 500). So it's a protected investment that can provide some participation in the upside of the market.

There are ads on the radio suggesting these indexed annuities are a panacea. You get the upside of the market without the risk! But they may not be telling you the full story.

Most index annuities these days are capped in some way (it varies from product to product). For example, you could have one based on the S&P 500 where the cap is 5%. If the index is down for the year, you lose nothing. If the index is up 3%, you get 3%. If the index is up 5%, you get 5%. But if the index is up 10%, 20%, or 30%, you still get 5%.

Also, stock returns are based on two things: price appreciation (the amount the share price changes over time), and dividends. Dividends are cash payments that some stocks provide to shareholders. Typically with fixed index annuities, the return is based only on the price appreciation of the index. You do not receive any credit for dividends the stocks in the index pay. So in essence, the lost dividend is a cost you incur to insure the investment.

Fixed index annuities are often touted as a risk-free way to fully participate in the stock market. The fine print might reveal that's not really what they offer. Again, if someone tries to sell you something without describing how it *really* works . . . run, Forrest, run!

Investment Accounts

There is a somewhat bewildering array of different accounts that can be used to tuck money away for retirement. If we tried to describe them all in detail, you might pass out from boredom before we made it to the end of the chapter. But it is important to understand the main categories of investment accounts, their basic rules, and the way they are taxed.

Taxable Accounts

Income and dividends in bank accounts and basic investment accounts are taxable in the year they are incurred (unless the investments themselves—municipal bonds or annuities, for example—enjoy some sort of tax advantage).

Taxability is a key point that we find can be confusing for some investors. In some cases there are tax advantages associated with a particular type of account, most notably retirement accounts such as IRAs or 401(k)s. On the other hand there are certain types of investments—for example, tax-free municipal bonds—that receive beneficial tax treatment.

A fancy term you may come across for taxable accounts is **nonqualified**, meaning they receive no preferential tax treatment.

A deep dive into the tax treatment of various accounts and investments is beyond the scope of this book. However, we do want to stress that proper tax strategy can have a big impact when it comes to saving money for retirement and when drawing income from your investments during retirement. The advice of a good CPA or investment advisor—or better yet a CPA and investment advisor who coordinate their efforts on your behalf—can be very valuable in this regard.

Retirement Accounts

There are certain investment accounts that the government has blessed with tax advantages. Most notable among these are the traditional Individual Retirement Account (IRA), the 401(k), and the Roth versions of both of those. Note that these aren't actually investments by themselves. They are just legal structures that can house a variety of different types of investments (stocks, bonds, mutual funds,and so forth).

The traditional IRA is the granddaddy of retirement accounts. Written into law back in 1974, IRAs now hold more than $5 trillion worth of American retirement savings.[5] Anyone under the age of 70½ who has earned income can contribute to one (although whether the contribution is tax-deductible depends on your income level and whether you participate in a plan at work[6]). As of 2018, the limit for annual contributions is $5,500, or $6,500 if you are 50 or older. You can contribute directly to an IRA, or roll money into one from another plan, such as a 401(k), after changing jobs or retiring. (Look into something called the "age 55 rule" before rolling into an IRA if you retire between the ages of 55 and 59 ½, as it may impact you decision making.) Typically you receive a tax deduction for contributing to an IRA, and then you don't pay taxes again on the money until you take it out. You pay a 10% penalty, in addition to taxes, if you pull money out of retirement accounts prior to age 59½ (with some exceptions[7]).

Speaking of taking money out, starting at age 70½ the IRS makes you remove money from a traditional IRA each year (so they can tax it). The amount is calculated by taking your life expectancy—per IRS tables—and dividing the end-of-year balance of your IRA(s) by that amount. Initially the Required Minimum Distribution (RMD) is about 3.6% of the value of all of your IRA money, and the percentage increases a bit each year. Do not mess around with this distribution . . . a 50% penalty applies on any money you should have taken out but didn't! There is some complexity surrounding the first time you take the RMD, so do your research or consult an advisor as you approach age 70½.[8] The money you take out each year (and the tax implications) should be considered as part of your financial plan.

So-called **qualified plans** are retirement accounts that receive preferential tax treatment. The 401(k) is the most common form, although there are several others that work in a similar fashion (for example, 403(b) plans are used by public school teachers and employees of some nonprofits). There are various differences among plans such as contribution limits, and whether or not contributions are made by the employer, the employee, or both. For the most part, they all offer some sort of tax benefit for contributing, and then the growth of the investments is sheltered from taxes until you pull the money back out.

Roth IRA and Roth 401(k) accounts receive an entirely different tax treatment. With a Roth you don't get a tax deduction when you put money in, but the money grows tax free for the rest of your life (and your heirs can let it grow tax-free for a while as well). Calculations can be made to help you figure out whether a Roth IRA or traditional IRA will be better for you in the long run, but those calculations require a bit of guesswork as to what tax laws will look like in the future. One un-mathematical way of looking at it is to ask yourself if Future You will thank Current You for choosing a Roth, because Current You dealt with the taxes so that Future You doesn't have to. Note that you do not have to worry about taking distributions beginning at age 70½ with this type of plan . . . the government has already taxed the money so it isn't in as much of a hurry for you to take it out.

In our experience as advisors, we've found that Americans who accumulate significant wealth for retirement primarily do so using some combination of the following:

- Saving effectively over a long period of time in a retirement plan

- Owning a business

- Owning real estate

- Inheriting money

Everyone, especially those to whom items 2 through 4 do not apply, should consider using the power of tax-advantaged retirement plans to build a nest egg for retirement.

Are You Going It Alone or Should You Hire an Advisor?

One of the decisions you want to make as you prepare for retirement is whether to go it alone or work with an investment advisor. As advisors we are obviously biased when it comes to this topic. That said, we will try to give you the lay of the land regarding your options and will discuss some of the pros and cons of working with an advisor.

Hiring an investment advisor involves a cost. It varies, but a typical arrangement is a 1% or so fee on your investment assets per year. Advisory fees can add up to serious bucks over time. These days, resources are available that will allow you to manage your own investments, so you need to give some thought to whether you want to pay someone for help or not.

You should consider whether your rate of return will be the same or better if you manage your portfolio by yourself. It is possible to provide yourself with returns that match or exceed those provided by an investment advisor. If you apply sound investment principles and are patient, you can be successful in this.

The problem with going it alone is that for many people it leads to subpar results. Vanguard, a company that perhaps has done more than any other to empower individual investors, estimates that an investment advisor following best practices can add 3% to average annual returns.[9] That somewhat stunning estimate is largely based on the unfortunate reality that individual investors, as we have discussed, often buy and sell investments at the wrong time.

Another consideration, aside from investment performance, is whether you want to offload all of the time and effort that goes into successful financial management. A good wealth manager will guide

"I'm worried about my investments. My broker has stopped quoting Warren Buffett and started quoting Jimmy Buffet."

you in trust and estate planning, charitable giving, tax and cash flow planning, insurance and asset protection, and the coordination of input from the various other professionals you work with (accountants, attorneys, insurance providers, and so forth).

Unfortunately, although most advisors hold themselves out as broad-scope financial planners, in reality most do not provide that depth of service. So if you want to work with a financial advisor, you need to be careful about who you choose. With that in mind, let's take a look at the types of advisors there are out there, and then we'll talk about the common attributes of good ones.

The world of investment advisors can be broken down as follows:

Wirehouse brokerage—These are the largest investment firms: Merrill Lynch, Morgan Stanley, UBS, and Wells Fargo. Their size allows them to offer a very broad menu of services including investment banking, traditional banking and lending, investment management, and more. All wirehouses are publicly traded companies, and face heightened regulatory scrutiny in the wake of the 2008 financial crisis.

Regional brokerage—Regionals also tend to offer a broad spectrum of services (usually with the exception of traditional banking), but are smaller companies with operations concentrated in certain areas of the country. There is some variety to the ownership structure of regional firms (public, private, employee-owned).

Independent financial planner—While an independent planner will typically clear (meaning settle transactions and maintain securities) through a large brokerage such as

Charles Schwab or LPL, these are individual businesses. Independent firms can consist of a single planner, or a collaboration of thousands. RIAs (Registered Investment Advisors) are independents who are compensated exclusively through fees and do not offer commission-based products. They pride themselves on acting as fiduciaries (more on that subject in a bit).

Insurance company representative—Many insurance companies maintain financial planning operations. Their investment recommendations tend to focus on "packaged" solutions, such as mutual funds and in particular insurance-based investments (life insurance and annuities).

Bank representative—It is common for banks to have an investment advisor on staff to help the bank's clients make investment decisions.

Family office—At the upper end of the market (typically $100 million of investable assets and above), families may hire a manager or team that focuses exclusively on the handling of their financial affairs. Alternately, a multi-family office may handle a relatively small number of high-net-worth clients. For those with the means, this approach provides a very personalized and comprehensive level of service.

A hot topic of the moment is whether financial advisors should, in the course of providing advice, act as **fiduciaries**. This is a legal concept that impacts the way they are able to charge investors.

Essentially, being a fiduciary means that advisors must act at all times in the best interest of investors when providing advice. That sounds like an unequivocally good thing, right? Maybe not, once you filter it through the vagaries of the legal system. There is some concern that the fiduciary requirement will lead to less advice being available to investors, particularly those who don't have large portfolios.

....

Paying for investment advice

There are different ways to pay for advice. Many advisors charge a fee based on the size of the assets they manage. Fees often fall somewhere between 1% and 2% of the assets under management, although they can be lower, particularly in the case of multimillion-dollar portfolios. Alternately, some planners may charge a flat annual fee, and some charge on an á la carte basis depending on the services provided (several thousand dollars for a financial plan, for example). Some advisors charge commissions on a per-transaction basis (annuities have commissions built into them, which accounts for some of the high costs), and some are paid by a mix of commissions and fees.

The advantage of the fee-based model is that it ties the compensation of the advisor to the success of the client's portfolio (the more it grows, the more the advisor is paid), and it removes any incentive for the advisor to drive up compensation through unnecessary transactions.

....

Advisors can either be sole practitioners (perhaps backed by one or more staff people), or they can work as part of a team. There are great sole practitioners out there, but teams have become more common. Teams have the advantage of continuity and shared workload. If one advisor is on vacation, retires, or is otherwise not available, a team that shares a strong process can continue to provide uninterrupted service.

Advisor credentials should also be considered. The investment industry has been experiencing "credential inflation" of late, as more and more accreditations have been invented, some of dubious merit. Here are some of the more well-established and recognized financial credentials:

CFP® (Certified Financial Planner™): The primary credential for financial planning. Attaining the CFP® requires study and testing in seven categories, followed by a comprehensive exam that only about 50%–70% of applicants are able to pass.[10]

CFA® (Chartered Financial Analyst™): The most mathematically rigorous of the leading credentials, it covers subjects like portfolio structure and corporate accounting. The testing is notoriously difficult.

CPA (Certified Public Accountant): The accounting profession's standard of competence. It is a title with legal standing, requiring experience along with rigorous study and testing.

ChFC® (Chartered Financial Consultant®): A financial planning designation common among insurance agents, it includes even more coursework than the CFP®, but without the comprehensive exam.

CLU® (Charted Life Underwriter): The most recognized credential specific to insurance. It requires completion of five courses (without a comprehensive exam).

PFS (Personal Financial Specialist): Offered by the American Institute of Certified Public Accountants (AICPA). A PFS is a Certified Public Accountant (CPA) with additional expertise in financial and wealth management.

Credentials don't guarantee that an advisor is any good, but the cost, time, and difficulty in obtaining some of the more rigorous ones can help to weed out the riffraff a bit.

You should also consider the amount of experience an advisor has. When it comes to experience, of course, the more the better. You want to work with someone who has seen their share of serious bear markets, because nothing imparts wisdom quite like a disaster.

Lousy advice is certainly not worth paying for, and it's not always easy to recognize good advisors from bad. Plus, resources are available these days that allow investors to successfully go it alone if they are willing to dedicate time to financial planning and can be diligent about their investment approach.

If you want to work with an advisor, do your homework. Check out the website of any advisors or firms you are considering; look up their complaint history on FINRA Broker Check. Seek referrals from friends, family and other trusted associates. And finally, interview a number of them. Compare their processes, and the vibe you get when you meet them. Ideally you are establishing a long-term relationship built on trust, so you want to seek competence as well as a comfort level with their personality.

Drill down on the specific list of services they offer. Don't fall for terms like "comprehensive" or "holistic" unless they are backed up with a specific list of services that fit the description. A good advisor should follow a detailed process that helps lead you to financial success. Ask any advisor you interview to describe their process in detail. If they fail that test, look elsewhere.

Protecting Your Future

You just worked your way through two chapters on the subject of money and investing, yet we barely scratched the surface of the topic. Of course, this book isn't about investing, it's about finding happiness in retirement, and finances are just one part of it. Hopefully we have framed things in a way that will help guide further exploration. In the final chapter, "The Retirement Happiness Map," we will describe next steps to take toward securing your financial future, including the crafting of a financial plan.

Always remember that money is not the goal. Happiness is the goal. Money is just a helpful tool that may or may not help you to achieve it.

Endnotes

1   History Says There's a 99% Chance Stock Market Returns Will Be Subpar From Here. https://www.cnbc.com/2017/07/31/theres-a-99-percent-chance-stock-market-returns-will-be-subpar-from-here.html

2   The Case for Managed Futures in a Bull Market. https://seekingalpha.com/article/2130493-the-case-for-managed-futures-in-a-bull-market

3   SPIVA U.S. Scorecard. https://us.spindices.com/documents/spiva/spiva-us-year-end-2016.pdf

4   Trends in the Expenses and Fees of Funds, 2016. https://www.ici.org/pdf/per23-03.pdf

5   GAO Report on Individual Retirement Accounts. https://www.gao.gov/products/GAO-15-16

6   Who Can Contribute to a Traditional IRA. http://money.cnn.com/retirement/guide/IRA_traditional.moneymag/index3.htm?iid=EL

7   Hardships, Early Withdrawals and Loans. https://www.irs.gov/retirement-plans/hardships-early-withdrawals-and-loans

8   Retirement Topics—Required Minimum Distributions. https://www.irs.gov/retirement-plans/plan-participant-employee/retirement-topics-required-minimum-distributions-rmds

9   Vanguard's Advisors Alpha. https://advisors.vanguard.com/iwe/pdf/FASQAAAB.pdf

10 CFP® Examination Statistics. https://www.cfp.net/news-events/research-facts-figures/cfp-examination-statistics

CHAPTER 5

Navigating the Maze of Medicare

LegacyHealthInsurance.com

In the theater of confusion, knowing the location of the exits is what counts. — Mason Cool

About three months before their 65th birthday, most Americans will be contacted by Medicare. Those receiving Social Security at the time will be automatically enrolled, while all who are eligible will receive an Initial Enrollment Questionnaire. Most will want to enroll, although some exceptions are made for those with employer-paid coverage that meets certain criteria. The more educated you are about Medicare before you get that form in the mail, the better.

Healthcare costs are one of largest expenses you'll have in retirement, so the choices you make about Medicare can have a profound impact on your health and financial security as you age. A Harvard University study showed that 62 percent of personal bankruptcies in the US were the result of medical expenses.[1] Stunningly, 72 percent of those people had health insurance. Running out of money is a huge fear for most retirees, and going bankrupt or becoming a financial burden for your children is definitely not an example of "winning."

Our intent with this chapter, as with much of the book, is not to take a deep dive into a very complex subject. Rather, we will explain the basics and some key considerations, describe the decisions you need to make, and point you in the direction of resources you can access to move forward with your planning. With Medicare enrollment, you have to choose how to structure what will most likely be one of the biggest costs you have to deal with for the rest of your life.

Tackling Medicare takes some effort, but it is worthwhile to spend some time and get it right. Your Medicare coverage choices will impact expenses of course, but also the degree of freedom you have in selecting healthcare providers. You will need to weigh whether minimizing costs or maximizing choice is your bigger priority.

The Story of Medicare

Medicare is a social program aimed at helping older Americans shoulder the burden of rising healthcare costs. It began in 1965 with a bill signed into law by President Lyndon B. Johnson. The intention was to help retirees and individuals with disabilities pay for a portion of their healthcare. Notice the word *portion*. Medicare was never intended to provide free healthcare benefits. Instead, the goal was for the program to pay 80 percent and beneficiaries to pay a 20 percent share. The program has evolved significantly over the years and now provides critical support to millions of Americans.

You've probably heard reference to the different "parts" of Medicare. There are four main components, known as Part A, Part B, Part C and Part D.

- **Part A** and **Part B**, *combined*, represent what is called Original Medicare. Part A covers hospital expenses, and Part B covers medical insurance. These two components represent Medicare's seminal intention: to help with expenses when someone goes to the hospital or sees a doctor.

- **Part C**—called **Medicare Advantage**—is composed of privately offered health insurance plans intended to mimic Parts A and B. Many plans offer prescription drug coverage and some non-traditional healthcare services (more about this later).

- Medicare **Part D** was added more recently (2006) and provides outpatient prescription drug coverage.

Over time, people with Original Medicare came to want coverage for the gap between what healthcare actually cost and what Medicare pays for. So **Medigap insurance** (also called supplemental coverage) was invented. Today, Original Medicare covers around 62% of total healthcare expenses.[2] Medigap coverage is one way to get help with the other 38 percent.

Figure 5.1 (next page) provides a good summary of the program and what is covered under each part:

Figure 5.1: The Different Parts of Medicare

Medicare Part A (Hospital Insurance) helps cover
- Inpatient care in hospitals
- Skilled nursing facility care
- Hospice care
- Home healthcare

Medicare Part B (Medical Insurance) helps cover
- Services from doctors and other healthcare providers
- Outpatient care
- Home healthcare
- Durable medical equipment
- Many preventive services

Medicare Part C (Medicare Advantage)
- Includes all benefits and services covered under Part A and Part B
- Usually includes Medicare prescription drug coverage (Part D) as part of the plan
- Run by Medicare-approved private insurance companies that follow rules set by Medicare
- Plans have a yearly limit on out-of-pocket costs for medical services
- May include extra benefits and services that aren't covered by Original Medicare, sometimes for an extra cost

Medicare Part D (Medicare prescription drug coverage)
- Helps cover the cost of prescription drugs
- Run by Medicare -approved drug plans that follow rules set by Medicare
- May help lower your prescription drug costs and help protect against higher costs in the future

Data source: Medicare &You, the National Medicare Handbook 2018

Medicare.gov is a very good resource, as is the *Medicare & You* handbook you'll find there.[3] You will want to download the most recent edition of the handbook from the website or call 1-800-MEDICARE to request a paper version. The document is quite long, but is written in plain English, and it is the bible of the Medicare system (it's where we got several of the charts you'll see in this chapter).

Your Two Options: Original Medicare vs. Medicare Advantage

The healthcare costs for people over the age of 65 in the United States are primarily covered either by Original Medicare (meaning Parts A and B, perhaps with Part D and/or a Medigap supplement)—**OR** they are covered by a Medicare Advantage Plan (Part C).

Figure 5.2 from Medicare.gov shows the two paths you can go down, and the ancillary decisions you need to make as a result.

The difference between Original Medicare and Medicare Advantage boils down to two key areas: (1) cost and (2) options for care. Other considerations are whether you travel a lot, and where you expect to receive your care.

Figure 5.2: The Two Medicare Coverage Options

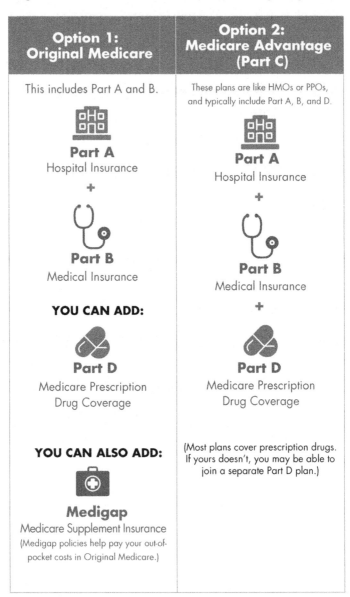

Data source: *Centers for Medicare & Medicaid Services, Medicare & You 2018*

In the following subsections, we'll compare Original Medicare and Medicare Advantage based on six components:

    a. Which providers you can use

    b. How premiums work (including potential increases)

    c. Co-pays and deductibles

    d. Obtaining care when you travel

    e. Wellness visits and preventive measures

    f. Drug coverage

A) Which Providers You Can Use

Depending on which doctors and hospitals you use, this decision may be fairly easy to make. Simply put, **Original Medicare will let you see almost any doctor you want, while Medicare Advantage limits you to in-network physicians**. The difference resides in how hospitals and doctors are paid.

Original Medicare is a fee-for-service program. That means Medicare will reimburse any doctor or hospital for the services you use. Because of this fee-for-service model, you can go to any doctor or hospital you like, as long as they accept Medicare. (Don't worry—9 in 10 doctors participate.[4])

By contrast, Medicare Advantage plans are issued by private insurance companies. The plans keep costs down by restricting you to physician networks or coordinated care groups like HMOs and PPOs. They must provide at least the same coverage as Original Medicare

(Part A & B), and can provide additional coverage like dental and vision. Some even go as far as covering gym memberships and other holistic care. Medicare Advantage plans receive money from Medicare for each of their participants (about $10,000 per participant annually[5]), no matter how much it costs to keep that person healthy.

The obvious advantage with Original Medicare is that you have the ability to choose your providers no matter where they practice. It might not mean a lot to you now, but imagine if you have a serious illness in the future. What if the specialist you want to see is in another State or is out of network? With Original Medicare, you have more freedom of choice.

With Medicare Advantage, if you want to see someone out of network, you could face significant out-of-pocket costs. This is something to really think about. Settling for a physician because he or she is in your network, as opposed to them being the best doctor for you, is serious stuff. Especially if you are dealing with a major medical issue.

Let's look at an example to see how Medicare Advantage works: Jane is in picture-perfect health and has few medical needs beyond routine care. John, however, is battling diabetes. As a result, he sees a number of specialists and has an expensive regimen of care and medications. Medicare will pay the private insurer who administers the Medicare Advantage plan exactly the same amount for Jane as they will for John, even though Jane did not generate much cost to her plan and John was far more expensive. From the Medicare Advantage insurer's perspective, there are millions of reasons ($) why they want to keep their subscribers healthy. The fewer trips to the doctor people make, the more money the insurer keeps.

Some evidence suggests that patients who use a network of physicians have better health outcomes.[6] The network should know your history better than a scattered group of doctors. Moreover, there should be less redundancy in testing and treatment because your providers are able to share your health information easily with one another. The insurance company's incentive to keep costs low may result in a higher focus on preventive care than you might experience with Original Medicare.

As mentioned before, the big downside with Medicare Advantage is the cost if you go outside the selected network. Reflect on what is more important to you: freedom to choose healthcare providers, or working with a coordinated network of providers at what might be a lower cost.

B) Premiums

The good news is that Medicare Part A is free as long as you qualify—and there is a good chance that you do. You are eligible for Part A if you are 65 or older and you or your spouse worked and paid Medicare taxes for at least 10 years.

Medicare Part B premiums must be paid by all enrollees, even those who choose a Medicare Advantage plan instead of Original Medicare. The price of that premium depends on your income. For 2018 the standard monthly cost is $134. From there it goes higher based on your modified adjusted gross income (MAGI). MAGI in this context—there are other versions—is your regular AGI (found on your tax return) plus any tax-exempt interest income. The chart below illustrates the difference in Part B premiums based on MAGI. Note that payments are based on tax returns on file with the IRS, meaning the figures typically represent your income from your return from a prior year—in this case, the MAGI from a 2016 return filed in 2017 is used to determine 2018 payments.

Figure 5.3: Part B Premiums for 2018

| If your yearly income in 2016 was... | | | You pay each month (in 2018) |
File individual tax return	File joint tax return	File married & separate tax return	
$85,000 or less	$170,000 or less	$85,000 or less	$134
above $85,000 up to $107,000	above $170,000 up to $214,000	Not applicable	$187.50
above $107,000 up to $133,500	above $214,000 up to $267,000	Not applicable	$267.90
above $133,500 up to $160,000	above $267,000 up to $320,000	Not applicable	$348.30
above $160,000	above $320,000	above $85,000	$428.60

To use this chart, find your filing status (individual, joint, or married filing separately) then move down to the row that corresponds to your income. The last column tells you what your premium would be as of 2018. (Source: https://www.medicare.gov/your-medicare-costs/part-b-costs/part-b-costs.html).

••

What if your MAGI drops?

Your premium in a given year is based on your MAGI from the *prior* year. If you expect a drop in income based on one of the following reasons, you can notify the Social Security Administration and request a lower premium:

- You married, divorced, or became widowed
- You or your spouse stopped working or reduced your work hours
- You or your spouse lost income-producing property because of a disaster or other event beyond your control
- You or your spouse experienced a scheduled cessation, termination, or reorganization of an employer's pension plan
- You or your spouse received a settlement from an employer or former employer because of the employer's closure, bankruptcy, or reorganization

••

The bullet points in the sidebar and the following are copied verbatim from the 2018 version of the publication "Medicare Premiums: Rules for Higher Income Beneficiaries"[7]: *You should consider working with a tax professional to make sure there are no surprises with your Part B premium. A high MAGI in a given year can impact your Medicare premium for several years.*

Medicare Advantage premiums

As noted, everyone is required to pay Part B premiums. Medicare Advantage users must pay an *additional* premium, which varies by plan. It's important to shop around because even plans offering the exact same benefits can have different premiums. Remember, Medicare

Advantage plans are run by private insurers, and each can set a different rate. Remember too that premiums are only part of the picture—you also have to consider deductibles and co-pays (more on that later), which also vary.

Typically, Medicare Advantage is less expensive for most people. That is, the total cost to Medicare Advantage users—which includes the Part B premium, plus any extra premiums for the plan, plus out-of-pocket expenses for co-pays, etc.—is generally lower than the total cost for Original Medicare users (which can include costs for Medigap and Part D coverage).

Premium cost increases

The monthly Part B premium does rise over time. These increases tend to be fairly modest, because Medicare is a government program and it needs to be accessible for Americans of all means. Being a government program suggests a certain amount of stability; Original Medicare cannot suddenly withdraw coverage from participants. The same is not true for Medicare Advantage. Since Medicare Advantage plans are privately run, premium increases can vary more widely than those of Medicare Part B. Moreover, Medicare Advantage plans are not guaranteed to be offered year after year. They can be withdrawn from your state by the companies that manage them.

If you favor stability in pricing and provider choice, then Original Medicare may be better for you. If lower costs out of the gate are of paramount importance, then Medicare Advantage is typically a better fit (again, depending on your particular needs).

C) Co-pays and Deductibles

The other costs to consider when deciding between Medicare and Medicare Advantage are deductibles and co-pays. These are your out-of-pocket expenses. For Medicare Part A, your deductible and co-pays are based on any time you spend in the hospital. This can get a little tricky, so please visit https://www.medicare.gov/coverage/hospital-care-inpatient.html for details. Be mindful that when you go to the hospital, you must be very clear about whether you are admitted or are under observation. Medicare Part A will kick in when you are considered admitted, not when you are under observation. This will impact the amount of coverage you will have while in the hospital and therefore the cost you may be responsible for.

Deductibles and co-pays for Part B under Original Medicare are a bit more straightforward. First, you are responsible for a yearly deductible of $183, then Medicare will pay 80% of costs and your co-pay is 20%. For example, if your first visit to a doctor in a calendar year costs $283, you are responsible for the $183 deductible, then Medicare will pay $80 and you will pay $20 for the remaining $100. In any future visits, the 80/20 split will apply between Medicare and you.

Medicare Advantage is different in that co-pays are a flat rate rather than a percent. This makes it easier to project your out-of-pocket spending for a given year. But because private insurance companies have discretion over your co-pay, there is the potential for more price fluctuation from year to year.

....

Summary: Costs and financial exposure risks for Original Medicare and Medicare Advantage

The most significant risk you face if you choose Original Medicare over Medicare Advantage is that Original Medicare has no out-of-pocket limit. This means a catastrophic health issue can become a catastrophic financial issue. If you choose Original Medicare, you should consider purchasing supplemental insurance commonly known as a Medigap plan. Medigap policies can help cover deductibles and co-pays to protect you from large financial outlays, and therefore protect you from financial ruin.

In contrast, all Medicare Advantage policies are required to have an out-of-pocket maximum for participants when they choose in-network care, which is a huge safety net. Buyer beware, though . . . there is no out-of-pocket maximum for out-of-network care.

Remember that your spouse and your family may also be impacted by the coverage decisions that you make. And bear in mind not only your current health issues, but other problems you may encounter down the road.

....

D) Obtaining Care When You Travel

Travel and retirement are like peas and carrots—they just go together. When we talk to clients about their retirement plans, travel is almost always part of the picture. It is important to understand how travel can impact your health insurance if you get sick when you are away from home. In the United States, Original Medicare will cover you wherever you go as long as the doctor or hospital accepts Medicare. But remember, Medicare Advantage plans will penalize you if you see a doctor out of network, and most doctors out of your state will be out of your network. Thankfully, all plans cover emergency or urgent care anywhere in the country.

Travel overseas is another story. One of our client couples has children that live out of the United States, and they visit them regularly. They had two options for coverage while out of the country. Under Original Medicare, they could buy a Medigap policy that would cover a majority of their costs. Under Medicare Advantage, they would have to buy a supplemental travel policy every time they went abroad. Our clients felt that the supplemental Medicare Advantage was the way to go because they were traveling overseas just one or two times a year for a month at a time. If you are traveling abroad frequently, then the permanent Medigap policy may be less expensive. Additional details about overseas coverage can be found here: https://www.medicare.gov/coverage/travel-need-health-care-outside-us.html.

E) Wellness Visits and Preventive Measures

Original Medicare now offers an annual wellness visit (at no cost) that can help you benchmark your health from year to year, with the goal of helping you to avoid getting sick. Certain other preventive measures such as screenings, vaccines, and counseling may be fully covered as well. Medicare Advantage plans must fully cover all preventive services that are provided at no cost under Original Medicare, and may cover some others as well.

Original Medicare will not pay for a gym membership, but some Medicare Advantage plans will. Are any non-traditional wellness practices important to you? For example, do you see a chiropractor, an acupuncturist, or a naturopathic doctor? Some of these services are covered by Medicare Advantage plans, but they are not covered by

Original Medicare (except for chiropractic care, which is covered only when deemed medically necessary).

While Original Medicare does not offer extra preventive services, some Medigap policies do. These relatively new versions are called Innovative Medigap policies and are offered in 21 states. We will talk about Medigap options shortly.

F) Drug Coverage

The cost of prescription medications in the U.S. is staggering. Spending for drugs in the U.S. far exceeds that of other high-income countries,[8] and unless something is done, costs will continue to climb. The idea that a commonly used chemotherapy drug, Revlimid, can cost on average $182,972 per year[9] is pretty incredible.

Currently drug price negotiations are handled by the private insurers that offer Medicare Part D drug plans. Many believe better savings could be had if the government itself handled negotiations with pharmaceutical companies, leveraging the full buying power of the American public. On the other hand, there is some concern that squeezing too much profit out of the drug business will stifle innovation and new drug development. It is a complex topic that we won't wade into, but suffice to say that rising drug prices are a serious concern for all Americans, especially retirees.

Most Medicare Advantage plans include prescription drug coverage. If yours does not, or if you choose Original Medicare, you should consider an optional Medicare Part D prescription drug plan. You will pay an additional monthly premium, but paying a little extra each month in premiums can prevent you from having to pay a lot more in prescription costs, especially as you get up higher in age or encounter a serious health problem. Frankly, given the stratospheric costs of some drugs, we consider some form of Part D a must. Bear in mind that if you delay signing up for Part D instead of signing up when you are first eligible, your monthly costs will be higher —forever—because you will be older when you enroll (there is more on enrollment later in this chapter). There are exceptions to this if you have something called "creditable coverage" from another source, but that is a complex subject we will not delve into. (Seek knowledge and help with the subject if you plan to delay enrolling in Part D because of you have other drug coverage.)

Like Medicare Advantage plans and Medigap supplemental plans, prescription drug plans are offered by private insurers, so you will have no shortage of marketing offers coming your way. Throw them all in the trash. You don't want to pick your plan based on a sales pitch, but rather on your personal circumstances, along with a bit of research.

In *Medicare for Dummies*, AARP Medicare expert Patricia Barry says that the right plan should be one that covers all the drugs that you are taking now, at the lowest cost, with the fewest hoops to jump through to get it.[10] Later in this chapter, we'll instruct you on how to do a healthcare assessment and prepare a list of all the medications you currently take, and in what dosage and frequency. No matter where you live, you most likely will have 25 or more prescription drug plans to choose from. Having a list of medications will help you whittle that list down to about two or three options that are best for you.

The good news is that you have the ability to change your Part D coverage each year without penalty, so if your prescription needs are different down the road, you can adjust accordingly.

By the way, *Medicare for Dummies* is a terrific resource. It provides explicit detail on all things Medicare, and goes far deeper than what we will cover in this chapter.

Medigap Policies

Original Medicare requires you to pay premiums, deductibles, and co-pays, and it has no out-of-pocket maximum. These costs can present a significant cramp in your lifestyle at best, and at worst can completely upend your well-planned retirement.

Medigap policies are the answer. They are supplemental policies offered by private insurers that cover a variety of the out-of-pocket costs you might face. Unlike the vast number of Medicare Advantage plans out there, Medigap has only 10 versions to choose from (like the Medicare parts, they are named with letters: A, B, C, D, F, G, K, L, M & N). No matter what private insurance company you buy your plan from, *they all are exactly the same in structure because they are regulated by Medicare*. So if you buy policy F from one insurer, it should be *exactly* the same as if you buy policy F from another insurer (with the exception of Innovative policies, which throw in a bit of extra coverage).

Figure 5.4 (next page) is from Medicare & Medicaid Services and illustrates the difference between the plans and what they cover. You need to decide what components of coverage are most important and least important to you, and then start whittling down which options you want to pursue in terms of getting quotes. For example, if foreign travel is not in your plans, then you could eliminate the options that provide foreign travel coverage.

Figure 5.4: Comparing Medigap Plans[11]

Medigap Benefits	Medigap Plans									
	A	B	C	D	F*	G	K	L	M	N
Part A co-insurance and hospital costs up to an additional 365 days after Medicare benefits are used up	Yes	Yes	Yes	Yes	Yes	Yes	Yes	Yes	Yes	Yes
Part B co-insurance or copayment	Yes	Yes	Yes	Yes	Yes	Yes	50%	75%	Yes	Yes***
Blood (first 3 pints)	Yes	Yes	Yes	Yes	Yes	Yes	50%	75%	Yes	Yes
Part A hospice care co-insurance or copayment	Yes	Yes	Yes	Yes	Yes	Yes	50%	75%	Yes	Yes
Skilled nursing facility care co-insurance	No	No	Yes	Yes	Yes	Yes	50%	75%	Yes	Yes
Part A deductible	No	Yes	Yes	Yes	Yes	Yes	50%	75%	50%	Yes
Part B deductible	No	No	Yes	No	Yes	No	No	No	No	No
Part B excess charge	No	No	No	No	Yes	Yes	No	No	No	No
Foreign travel exchange (up to plan limits)	No	No	80%	80%	80%	80%	No	No	80%	80%
Out-of-pocket limit	N/A	N/A	N/A	N/A	N/A	N/A	$5240	$2620	N/A	N/A

* Plan F also offers a high-deductable plan. If you choose this option, this means you must pay for Medicare-covered costs up to the deductible amount of $2,240 in 2018 before your Medigap plan pays anything.

** After you meet your out-of-pocket yearly limit and your yearly Part B deductible, the Medigap plan pays 100% of covered services for the rest of the calender year.

*** Plan N pays 100% of the Part B coinsurance, except for copayment of up to $20 for some office visits and up to a $50 copayment for emergency room visits that don't result in patient admission.

If you want to have your Part A deductible covered, then you'd need to look at plan options that include that benefit.

Be aware that there is some complexity involved if you want to change Medigap coverage. While you can sometimes make changes during the annual open enrollment window, you are not guaranteed access to other plans outside of the initial enrollment. Also, there can be issues if you initially elect Medicare Advantage and later want to switch to Original Medicare.

During initial enrollment you have access to any Medigap policy regardless of your health status. If you initially sign up for Medicare Advantage and later try to switch to Original Medicare, you will probably be subject to medical underwriting for Medigap coverage, and could be denied access for health reasons (some states have exceptions to this).

Some experts advise that you buy a Medigap policy with the most comprehensive set of benefits you can afford at initial enrollment, because upgrading in the future can be expensive.[12]

While the plans are the same, the premiums vary. Insurance companies can price premiums in three ways: community rating, issue-age rating, and attained-age rating. Visit medicare.gov to become familiar with the pricing models. You will likely find that most plans are based on attained age (meaning how old you are at the time of purchase). All plans are subject to price increases due to inflation even if they don't increase based on age.

Study the chart above to see what characteristics of a Medigap plan might be of interest to you. The Kaiser Family Foundation maintains a list of plans by state: www.kff.org/medicare/state0indicator/plans/?currenttimeframe=0.

You can also use the Medigap section of Plan Finder on Medi...
to shop for coverage: https://www.medicare.gov/find-a-plan/questions/medigap-home.
aspx.

Choosing an Option and Enrolling in Medicare

Now that you have a general sense of Medicare and its various
components, it's time to start working toward a decision about what
will be best for you.

Step 1: Start with a self-assessment of your health

There is one thing we are completely sure about when it comes to this
whole Medicare thing: the first step is to gather as much information
as you can about your current health status and healthcare needs. Each
decision you make, and each conversation you might have with people
who can give you advice about Medicare, will be based on your unique
healthcare situation.

You—and, if applicable, your spouse—should complete a **health
assessment** by filling in a form that describes everything about your
wellness and medical life. You record the doctors you see, any current
health issues, family medical history, and the medications you take (the
last is of particular importance). Think about it: you can't figure out how
to best cover your healthcare needs without first accurately describing
them.

You can download a healthcare assessment on the health and
wellness page of RetiredHappy.me. Fill it out in as much detail as you
can. Also, look at your list of doctors. Reach out to them to see if they

(1) accept Medicare and (2) are in or out of network for any Medicare Advantage plan you consider.

It is said that Michelangelo was once asked how he created his masterpiece of sculpture, and the artist replied: "It's easy. You just chip away the stone that doesn't look like David." In essence, we suggest that you start your search for the right Medicare plan with that concept in mind. The vast number of options makes it nearly impossible to compare all of the plans together, so you will be much better off if you can eliminate the ones that don't fit right from the beginning. Once you can winnow the options down, it becomes easier to make comparisons.

Step 2: Compare options

Choice and quality of care, cost, travel needs, and additional service options are all factors to consider when making your decision about what path to choose when it comes to Medicare. Table 5.A (next page) provides a summary of the discussion earlier in this chapter.

If you travel the country frequently and want freedom of choice, then Original Medicare is for you. If you love your community doctors and hospitals and seek a lower cost option, then Medicare Advantage might be better. It is not always easy to cross one or the other off the list. You might need to find a good Medicare Advantage policy option, then compare it with the benefits and costs you'd receive under Original Medicare plus a supplement (Medigap) and a prescription drug plan (Part D).

Table 5.A: Summary of Original Medicare vs. Medicare Advantage Features

Original Medicare	Feature	Medicare Advantage
There's no limit on how much you pay out-of-pocket per year (unless you have supplemental coverage).	**Cost**	Plans have a yearly limit on your out-of-pocket costs. If you join a Medicare Advantage Plan, once you reach a certain limit, you'll pay nothing for covered services for the rest of the year.
Medicare covers medical services and supplies in hospitals, doctors' offices, and other health care settings. Services are covered under Part A or Part B.	**Coverage***	Plans must cover all the services that Original Medicare covers. However, plans may also offer benefits that Original Medicare doesn't cover, such as vision, hearing, or dental services.
You can add a Medigap policy to help pay your out-of-pocket costs in Original Medicare (such as your deductible and co-insurance).	**Supplemental coverage**	It may be more cost effective for you to join a Medicare Advantage plan because your cost sharing is lower (or included). You can't use (and can't be sold) a Medigap policy if you're in a Medicare Advantage plan.
You'll need to join a Medicare Prescription Drug Plan to get drug coverage.	**Prescription drugs***	Most Medicare Advantage plans include drug coverage.
You can go to any doctor that accepts Medicare.	**Doctor and hospital choice**	You may need to use healthcare providers who participate in the plan's network. If so, find out how close the network's doctors or pharmacies are to your home. Some plans offer out-of-network coverage.

Original Medicare	Feature	Medicare Advantage
You can get a snapshot of the quality of care that health care providers (and facilities) give their patients by visiting Medicare.gov.	**Quality of care**	The Medicare Plan Finder at Medicare.gov/find-a-plan features star rating systems for Medicare plans.
Original Medicare generally doesn't cover care outside the U.S. You may be able to buy supplemental insurance that offers travel coverage.	**Travel**	Plans usually don't cover care you get outside of the U.S.
* If you have other types of health or prescription drug coverage, check to see how it works with the type of coverage you're considering before you make any decisions.		

Source: Centers for Medicare & Medicaid Services, Medicare & You 2018

With your medical information in hand, you can use the Medicare Plan Finder on Medicare.gov to research Medicare Advantage (called "Medical Health Plans" in the system), and Part D plans. This link takes you to the appropriate section: https://www.medicare.gov/find-a-plan/questions/home.aspx. Check out the video on the right of the page under the title "Step-by-step overview on how to complete a plan search." It's a pretty good tutorial provided in five lessons.

If you already have Medicare coverage, you can use the Personalized Search option; otherwise use General Search. *Medicare for Dummies* provides step-by-step instructions for using the system.

Based on your state and the medications you take, the Plan Finder will provide quotes on a variety of plans that you can then compare. It includes information about premiums, as well as deductibles and co-pays. It also shows an estimate of your annual costs with a given plan, and a number for the maximum out-of-pocket costs that you might face. Medicare also provides ratings for plans based on a star system (you can find an explanation of that system on the site).

There is a link next to each plan that will take you to a registration page once you decide on the coverage you want.

Step 3: Enroll in Medicare

One common misconception about Medicare is that everyone is enrolled automatically. That is not exactly the case.

It is true that individuals who are already receiving Social Security at age 65 will be automatically enrolled in Parts A and B. If that applies to you, about three months before your 65th birthday, you will receive a Medicare card and a letter explaining that you have been signed up. This is a nice service, but it can cause confusion. There are other choices you still have to make, including whether to use Medicare Advantage, whether to get a Medigap policy, and how to get prescription drug coverage.

But what happens if you are not taking Social Security at age 65? Then you have to self-enroll. If that's the case, you have a window of time to sign up for Medicare, which includes the month of your 65th birthday, as well as the three months prior and the three months after. **Enrolling during this window assures you will face no penalties and will not run the risk of spending time without healthcare coverage.**

As mentioned earlier, you will receive the Medicare Initial Enrollment Questionnaire in the mail about three months before your 65th birthday. You also have the option to complete that form, as well as the enrollment documents, online. Visit https://www.mymedicare.gov/registration.aspx and create an online account. Keep in mind, it must be three months before you are eligible for Medicare (the month of your 65th birthday) to six months after coverage begins in order for you to access all the forms. For assistance, you can call the 24-hour toll-free hotline: 1-800-633-4227.

If you continue to work beyond age 65 and have coverage at work, you may not need to sign up at that time. Instead, you might be able to continue coverage from your employer. Then whenever you leave work and lose healthcare coverage from the employer, you will have an opportunity—called Special Enrollment—to get into Medicare. This is a complex subject that we'll discuss in the next subsection.

General enrollment: If you miss your Initial Enrollment or Special Enrollment window, you must wait until the next General Enrollment period. This runs from January 1st to March 31st each year, with coverage beginning July 1st. Be careful: if you end up missing Initial or Special Enrollments, you can be left without coverage (possibly racking up medical bills) for months. Or even years if you continue to delay.

Delaying costs money, even if you don't encounter any medical bills. For each month that you wait beyond when you should have signed up, your monthly costs will increase *permanently*. This goes for all the various forms of coverage.

How Medicare Is Affected if You Work Past Age 65

In the not-so-distant past, people typically retired at 65, when full Social Security and full pension kicked in. Today, pensions have become rare, and the full retirement age for Social Security is creeping up to

67. People are commonly working well past 65. In fact, many have no interest in retiring at that age. This retirement evolution has led to a new question: who covers my healthcare costs when I work past 65?

If you plan on working past the traditional retirement age, you may be able to delay enrollment in parts of Medicare. While having options is great, it introduces a complicated concept: overlapping coverage. Your HR department may be able to walk you through this issue, but if not you'll need to do a bit of research on your own.

In the words of Patricia Barry in *Medicare for Dummies*:

"For as long as you're covered beyond age 65 by group health insurance provided by an employer for whom you or your spouse still actively work—and that employer has 20 or more employees—you can delay Part B enrollment until this employment or the health coverage ends (whichever comes first). At that point, you're entitled to a Special Enrollment period to sign up for Part B immediately and without penalty."

As noted, Medicare will send you the Medicare Initial Enrollment Questionnaire about three months before you become eligible (although we advise you to begin educating yourself on the subject long before that). The form allows you to notify Medicare if you intend to keep your employee coverage instead of activating Medicare Part B. Complete the form accurately and on time and you can save yourself a world of trouble. A properly completed questionnaire can ensure that your bills are paid promptly and by the right payer.

Make sure to keep Medicare informed when your coverage changes too. If you change jobs or retire, you should contact the Medicare

Benefits Coordination & Recovery Center (BCRC) to have your file updated. You can reach the BCRC at 1-855-798-2627 for assistance.

If you work for a small employer, Medicare is your primary insurance and you must enroll as usual, with one caveat: your employer plan may offer a supplement plan that goes beyond what Medicare offers. If your employer does offer a supplement, then you should compare it to buying a Medigap policy to see which is best.

Health Savings Accounts and Part A

Many employers today use high-deductible health plans. To help with the cost of the deductible, they typically offer a Health Savings Account as well.

We are big fans of Health Savings Accounts. They allow employees who participate in high-deductible plans to defer some of their salary, pretax, to pay for qualified healthcare expenses. If you are still employed and your employer offers an HSA, it may be in your best interest to fund it to the maximum allowable level for as long as you can. An HSA is a tax-free slush fund that you can use to pay for things like medical, dental, and vision expenses. Unlike other tax-advantaged accounts, you get a tax deduction for your contributions, *and* the money comes out tax-free for qualified expenses. Deduction on the way in, tax-free on the way out . . . win, win. (Be aware that taxes and penalties apply if you pull money out for non-medical purposes.)

If you contribute annually to a Health Savings Account, then you may want to consider delaying taking Medicare Part A. Why? If you are enrolled in Part A, then you *cannot* contribute to your HSA any longer, per IRS rules. Note that if you are taking Social Security at age 65, then you are automatically enrolled in Medicare Part A, which means no more HSA contributions for you. Our best advice here is to call your HSA provider directly to review your specific situation.

Getting Help

With Medicare, we think it is important to start by gaining a basic understanding of the program, and to gather your personal medical data, but after that it might be a good idea to seek some help. As referenced earlier, Medicare itself has a 24-hour toll-free hotline: 1-800-MEDICARE (1-800-633-4227). They can answer questions, and help you with the Plan Finder system.

If you or your spouse is still working, you might check with your company HR department. Some companies contract with providers such as Health Advocate that help employees nearing retirement to shop for a plan.

You can consult with your State Health Insurance Assistance Program (SHIP), a free counseling service that will have a wealth of information about the plans available where you live. Visit https://www.shiptacenter.org/ for contact information for your state's program. You can receive guidance from SHIP representatives in person or over the phone.

There are paid Medicare consultants such as Allsup Medicare Advisor that for a fee—typically measured in hundreds of dollars—will walk you through the search process. This might be a good choice if you don't mind paying a bit to offload much of the work.

Finally, you can seek out an insurance broker who will help you shop for plans. As opposed to dealing with a representative from an insurance company who can sell only their own employer's plans, brokers will have relationships with a number of different insurers (although likely not all available providers) and can help you shop among the ones they represent. Brokers can be very knowledgeable guides, but be aware that they may have a conflict of interest in that their compensation could be higher if you choose a more expensive plan. One way to find a broker is on the website of the National Association of Health Underwriters: https://forms.nahu.org/consumer/findagent2.cfm. Enter your zip code and a radius—say, 10 miles if you are near a major metro area—check the box for your state, and select "Medicare" from the list of services at the bottom of the page. Finally, click "Find NAHU Members" and hopefully a few options will pop up.

The Loss of Mike Foley: A cautionary Medicare story from Pat

While Kristin, my co-author, and I were writing this book, my father and our business partner, Mike Foley, passed away from a heart attack. My dad was a larger-than-life personality, renowned in the financial industry and among all who knew him for his warmth and humor.

What followed, in addition to being a personal tragedy, was a stark lesson in what happens when a loved one dies. First you need to plan a funeral, and in our case a rip-roaring Irish wake. Thankfully, all of us siblings (I am one of five) and our wonderful in-laws rallied together to make the arrangements. But that was only the beginning of the challenges we would face in the months that followed. Turns out no one was sure where the most recent copy of his will was located. We also weren't sure how many insurance policies there were. We didn't have access codes to get into online accounts. These are issues that point up the need for a family organizer, which we will describe in Chapter 8: Your Legacy.

All this was eventually resolved, but then we ran headlong into a Medicare saga.

If you work for a company that has more than 20 employees and you lose healthcare coverage (through separation of service or death), there is the option of moving onto something called COBRA. It is a temporary extension of the coverage provided under the company plan. There is an increase in cost because you become responsible for the part of the payment that used to be covered by the employer, but it may still be less expensive than Medicare.

In my mom's case, she and my dad had already paid their deductibles for the year (they carry over when you elect COBRA), and the monthly payments were going to be cheaper than Medicare. So she made the election. But something ended up slipping through the cracks, and it became a major problem.

As was so common in my parents' generation, my dad handled all the finances. As advisors, Kristin and I encounter this often with older clients. The husband passes away, and the wife—in the midst of incredible grief—suddenly finds herself in the unfamiliar position of being responsible for the household finances.

That is exactly what happened to my mom. My brother and sisters and I helped set up her bills on autopay, and were otherwise trying to transition her into financial independence. She assumed that her

COBRA insurance coverage was set up for autopay. We were handling bills as they came through to her in the mail. But the bill for her COBRA coverage happened to arrive while she away visiting family. As a result, her bill went past 30 days without being paid, and she lost her health insurance. Worse, she was told she would not be eligible for Medicare until the following year.

It is with no small sense of shame that I, a professional financial advisor, recount the story of my recently widowed mother losing her health insurance. How could we, how could I, have allowed this to happen? The answer is: chaos. The loss of a loved one is an inherently chaotic situation.

What ensued was a lesson in dealing with a giant healthcare conglomerate (the company that provided her COBRA coverage) and the even larger government agencies that administer the Social Security and Medicare systems. I will summarize the whole experience by saying that such organizations are neither flexible nor fun to deal with.

In the end it all worked out. My mom finally had her problem solved by someone in the Scranton (Penn.) office of the Social Security Administration. Scranton is a smallish city about 90 minutes north of Philadelphia. (Many will know it as the setting for the TV show "The Office.") There is a bit of a time-machine sense to a place like Scranton, where things feel—comfortably—a few years behind. This is where our family is from; my mom grew up in the area as the second oldest of nine kids.

As a result of her COBRA being cancelled, my mom was deemed to have been without any healthcare coverage for a period of months, and she had racked up considerable medical bills. After months of struggling to straighten things out, and countless phone calls to her healthcare provider and to the government, we ended up scheduling a visit to the Social Security office in Scranton so she could submit some paperwork. In a seeming miracle, the woman she met with in that office was able to straighten out the entire mess, securing Medicare coverage for my mom retroactive to her loss of COBRA.

There are a couple of lessons to be had in this story. One that Kristin and I already knew from prior experience with clients, and which we referenced earlier in the book, is that the level of assistance you get at local Social Security offices varies from place to pace. In fact, it can vary based on the individual government employee you randomly end up working with. You might get a friendly and experienced person who will be a terrific guide through the complexity of the system. You might get someone surly and unhelpful. So if you are struggling with an issue and aren't getting the help you need, consider trying again with a different person or a different office.

The other lesson is not as clear cut, and you should bear in mind I am largely basing this on a sample size of one. But it seems to me, given that you can get help from a Social Security office anywhere, that you might be better off finding one in a small town rather than a big city. Admittedly, aside from my mom's experience, I am basing this on a stereotype—which is that people in small towns tend to be nicer. But maybe, as well, people working in a small-town Social Security office aren't quite as busy and harried as in a big-city office. In any case, if you live in a big city and are hitting a wall in terms of getting help . . . consider setting an appointment a little farther afield.

Be Proactive About Medicare!

Every aspect of American healthcare is in flux. By the time you read this, some of the information we've provided may already be out of date. For example, the most popular supplement plan has long been Medigap Plan F, but recent legislation means F (and the somewhat similar Plan C) will no longer be available beginning in 2020.[13]

That said, some things tend to remain steady when it comes to Medicare:

1) Start planning early (around your 64th birthday), so you are prepared for open enrollment. Remember that delaying can cost you.

2) Begin with a detailed health assessment so you are armed with the necessary information to make a good decision.

3) Lean on Medicare.gov and the most recent version of the *Medicare & You* handbook as primary resources.

Beyond that, consider seeking assistance from the experts we described earlier. Healthcare expenses are a big burden for retirees, so make sure you put in the effort to maximize your Medicare results while containing costs as best you can.

We will revisit Medicare planning steps again at the end of the book when we walk you through the building of an action plan we call "The Retirement Happiness Map." In the meantime, let's talk about how to take care of yourself in an effort to increase retirement enjoyment while minimizing your healthcare needs.

Endnotes

1   Medical Bankruptcy in the United States, 2007: Results of a National Study. https://www.ncbi.nlm.nih.gov/pubmed/19501347

2   How Much Is Enough? Out-of-Pocket Spending Among Medicare Beneficiaries: A Chartbook," Henry J. Kaiser Family Foundation (July 2014)

3   You can access content of the handbook electronically at https://www.medicare.gov/medicare-and-you/medicare-and-you.html

4   There Is No Shortage of Doctors Willing to Take Medicare Patients. https://www.forbes.com/sites/howardgleckman/2013/12/18/there-is-no-shortage-of-doctors-willing-take-medicare-patients/#7868bd444816

5   *Get What's Yours for Medicare: Maximize Your Coverage, Minimize Your Costs* by Phillip Moeller, pg. 96. ISBN-13: 978-1501124006.

6   Less Intense Post-acute Care, Better Outcomes for Enrollees in Medicare Advantage Than Those in Fee-For-Service. https://www.healthaffairs.org/doi/abs/10.1377/hlthaff.2016.1027

7   https://www.ssa.gov/pubs/EN-05-10536.pdf

8   https://www.commonwealthfund.org/publications/issue-briefs/2017/oct/paying-prescription-drugs-around-world-why-us-outlier

9   *Get What's Yours for Medicare: Maximize Your Coverage, Minimize Your Costs* by Phillip Moeller, pg. 119. ISBN-13: 978-1501124006

10 *Medicare for Dummies* by Patricia Barry, pg. 199. ISBN-13: 978-1119348870

11 Source: https://www.medicare.gov/supplement-other-insurance/compare-medigap/compare-medigap.html

12 *Medicare for Dummies, 2nd Edition* by Patricia Barry. ISBN-13: 978-1119348870

13 How the 2020 Exit of Medigap Plan F Might Affect Your Healthcare Spending. https://www.forbes.com/sites/forbesfinancecouncil/2017/06/06/how-the-2020-exit-of-medigap-plan-f-might-affect-your-healthcare-spending/#6a45dc5d699a

CHAPTER 6

Move It!

Growing old should increase, not decrease, the value of human life. Just as with bourbon, it has the potential to smooth out roughness, add agreeable qualities, and improve character.

—Andrew Weil, M.D. (Healthy Aging: A Lifelong Guide to Your Physical and Spiritual Well-Being)

M ike Foley, co-author Pat's father (this book is dedicated to him), wasn't much for exercise. He took stabs at it from time to time, but it would be fair to say that he never truly absorbed it into his lifestyle. He passed away in 2017 at the age of 73, and during the seven or so years prior to his death he struggled with mobility. Mentally and from a personality perspective, he was always larger than life, a beloved man who left a positive mark on the world and the people around him. But in his final years, he had a hard time moving. He walked with a cane and feared the possibility of eventually needing to use a wheelchair. It's impossible to say if regular exercise would have allowed him to completely avoid the physical issues he struggled with, but it's fair to assume it might have made a difference.

In a study of contrasts, Pat's father-in-law is 74 at the time of this writing and is the picture of health. He volunteers as a ski patrolman in the winter, and (partly to keep in shape for skiing) he's a referee for youth field hockey and lacrosse games. At a recent lacrosse tournament, Pat marveled at how quickly his father-in-law ran up a steep hill to speak with him. There is no doubt: Pat's father-in-law is remarkably spry because exercise is part of his daily routine.

These examples are anecdotal, of course, but the cause and effect in each case is fairly clear and is well-backed by scientific data. How you will live later in life is likely to be greatly impacted by how physically active you are.

In this chapter and the next we will look at two major topics related to wellness: exercise and diet. We will also talk about how attitude can play a role, and the circular relationship between physical and mental wellness.

Whenever possible, we have tried to support our opinions in this book with sources and studies. Coming as we do from the world of investments, the concepts of probability, causation, and empirical evidence are important to us. Unfortunately, in the realm of health, as in the world of investing, sometimes you come across conflicting evidence, and there can be disagreement among learned experts.

Our non-scientific conclusion from researching exercise and diet is that there seems to be more consensus and clear data on the benefits of exercise than there is on the relative merits of different dietary approaches. It's not that diet is any less important from a health perspective, just that it's a more complicated topic because of the many variables that are involved.

We did come away from our research with clear beliefs about what constitutes a healthy diet, which we will share in the next chapter.

But first, let's talk about living long vs. living well, and how to take advantage of the good things that exercise can do for you.

We are not experts

Our comfort zone is not health and wellness. We are not medical doctors. We are not medical anything. But as advisors our job is to give counsel, and our approach is holistic, so information about staying healthy is very important to us.

Not being experts on wellness, we employed some of the tactics you will read about in Chapter 8 to take a deep dive into the topic. We read articles and studies and a number of good books. In particular, we found the following books enlightening (visit the Library page on RetiredHappy.me for a brief description of these and other great resources):

- *A Short Guide to a Long Life*, David B. Agus, M.D.
- *Healthy Aging*, Andrew Weil, M.D.
- *The Art and Science of Aging Well*, Mark E. Williams, M.D.
- *Younger Next Year*, Chris Crowly and Henry S. Lodge, M.D.

A number of consistent themes emerged during our research that formed the basis of the advice you are about to read. Remember, we lack any medical qualifications or expertise. So take this guidance with a big spoonful of "consult a doctor about all matters pertaining to your wellness." Seriously, that's not just a disclaimer. You should make sure to have a good general practitioner to quarterback your healthcare. Annual checkups are the cornerstone of a healthy lifestyle. If you don't already, now is the time to start making wellness a priority.

Longevity vs. Quality of Life

Let's start with a bit of bad news. No matter how hard you exercise and how much broccoli you eat, you might not be able to extend your life much beyond a certain point. Living longer is possible, but living extremely long is not the most likely outcome of eating well and exercising. Taking care of yourself is mostly about living *better*. An important concept when it comes to wellness later in life is the distinction between living long and living well.

> **TED Talk**
>
> *Laura Carstensen — Older people are happier*
>
> People are living longer, and happier, than ever before. Stress, worry, and anger all tend to diminish with age.

Living Longer

As far as living long, we are blessed to exist in a Golden Age of longevity. Aside from one notable dip during the influenza epidemic of 1918, American and global life expectancy has been on a steady rise for a very long time. A number of factors drive this result.[1] In particular, humans have become better at combating communicable diseases. We figured out that we should separate sewage from drinking water (yay!). We learned that doctors and nurses should wash their hands. We have vaccines. And we know that smoking is bad, so we are doing less of it. The result is increased life spans, as shown in Figure 6.1.

Figure 6.1: Increase in Life Expectancy

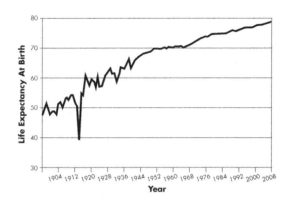

It is common to think of lifespan in terms of heredity, but studies suggest that behavior plays a bigger role.[2] In fact, 75% of how long we live may be determined by how we live rather than by who our parents are.

There are cultures where exceptional longevity is the norm, and research has been done on them that would presumably help us understand what it takes to live longer. But thus far there is no medical consensus that a certain diet or exercise regimen provides a high probability of living to 100 or beyond (although, see Dan Buettner's TED Talk for a discussion of the subject).

TED Talk

Dan Buettner—How to live to be 100+

A look at four different cultures where people tend to live to 100 and beyond, and the factors that help them get there.

Life expectancy for retired Americans today is well into the 80s.[3] And those statistics include a good number of people (majority?) who do not take care of themselves at all. So if you make it to retirement age, there is a good chance you will make it much further. However, the odds of doing that depend on how well you take care of yourself—that is, what you do to live well. If you do not take care of yourself, you may suffer an early death, as shown in Figure 6.2, which depicts a concept called Disability Adjusted Life Years.

Figure 6.2: Failure to Focus on Health Can Lead to Early Disability and/or Death

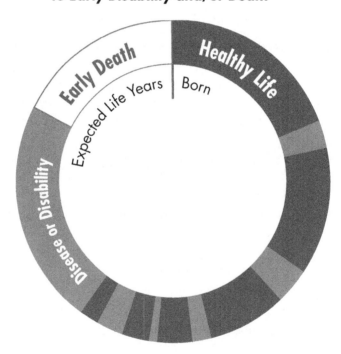

Living Well

While our longevity has been increasing, our progress in terms of quality of life is a more complicated question. In a sense—the book *Younger Next Year*[4] covers this idea in detail—we have become victims of our own success. Modern conveniences and the fact that we no longer need to hunt and forage for our food has allowed us to become a sedentary culture. That, and a calorie-laden diet has resulted in what has been described as an obesity epidemic. (You've probably heard all the bad news about obesity, but we will touch on the subject in Chapter 7.)

Fitness vs. weight

There is a tendency to think about fitness in terms of weight loss (which to be precise is really about losing fat). "I've got to lose a few pounds" is a common refrain. But while they are related, being fit and being thin are not necessarily the same things.

For example, *The Art and Science of Aging Well*[5] references a number of studies that suggest weight does not correlate to coronary heart disease, except at the extremes. In fact, it seems that fluctuations in weight may correlate more closely to heart issues than weight itself.[6]

In any case, do not think of fitness narrowly. It's not just about shedding fat . . . unless you fit the medical description of obese (which is typically defined as a measure of weight for a given height[7]). Bottom line: As long as you are not obese, focus on being fit rather than being thinner.

How do we square the fact that human longevity has been on a long uptrend with increasing levels of obesity and depression? This goes to the critical distinction between living long and living well. There are many factors involved, but one way to think of it is that better medicine has us living longer, while bad habits have us living worse.

As noted earlier, it's debatable whether you can find a way to live far beyond natural life expectancy. However, if you take care of yourself, you clearly have the ability to change your chances of dying *prior* to natural life expectancy. You can also reduce your odds of ending up disabled. Moreover, you can certainly improve your state of overall fitness—your quality of life—for however long you do remain on this Earth. But that will happen only if you take care of yourself, starting with regular exercise.

Why Should I Exercise?

Exercise is a somewhat easier subject than diet because the instructions are straightforward: **you should make exercise a part of your daily routine**. That is some of the most emphatic, unambiguous, unassailable advice we will give in this entire book, because the cause and effect relationship is so clear.

The book *Younger Next Year* sees the topic through the lens of human evolution. The authors make the point that through millions of years of development, our ancestors, from bacteria on, have survived via struggle and physical activity. Only in the past hundred years, a blink of the evolutionary eye, have we been able to provide for ourselves with a minimum of physical activity. Our bodies, the argument goes, are programmed to survive and thrive based on activity, or shut down and decay from the lack of it. And the modern lifestyle, absent a concerted effort to exercise, involves far too little activity. In short, the way we live these days programs us for decay.

The benefits of exercise are well documented. A recent study by Duke found that 20 minutes of moderate to vigorous exercise—even if broken up throughout the day—can notably decrease your odds of dying prematurely.[8] Results are truly dramatic for those who manage to exercise for 60 or 100 minutes per day (those numbers might sound daunting, but remember it does not have to be all at once). Moreover, you do not need to start out at that level. If you aren't currently exercising regularly, any amount of exercise will represent an improvement and can help you begin to form positive habits.

Whether or not you choose to make exercise part of your daily routine may be the single most important decision you make from this point forward in your life. Countless Americans are suffering from disease, are dying early, are using motorized carts to get around, are depressed, and are generally living less well than they should because of a failure to exercise.

"I guess I should start exercising again.
My treadmill sent me a friend request!"

It Hurts So Good — The Struggle of Exercise

We can lecture you, we can bombard you with facts, but whether or not you get up off the couch is up to you. Every year gyms across America swell in membership during the first three weeks of January with "New Year's Resolutionists." For those who go to the gym year-round, this annual migration is frustrating (the gym gets really crowded for a bit), but is also somewhat amusing to witness because of its perfect regularity.

That phenomenon illustrates two important things about exercise: 1) everyone knows they should exercise and most people at least take a stab at it, and 2) failure usually results.

If we knew the magic words that would help people easily take up exercise, we could leave the investment world and become famous fitness gurus. Which would be pretty sweet. Alas, we have no such words, so we will lay out the facts as we know them, and the rest is up to you.

Know that it is possible, if you stick with it long enough, to crave exercise. You can get to the point where you don't feel right if you go too far between workouts. It can become almost an addiction (in fact, it can become an actual addiction, but that's a subject for another book).

If you can make exercise so much a part of your routine that you miss it when you can't get it, you will have taken a great leap forward in the search for happiness in retirement.

Besides a positive physical response, exercise provides the emotional reward of knowing that you have accomplished something good. You walk out of the gym covered in sweat, simultaneously tired and exhilarated, patting yourself on the back for a job well done. Not a bad daily game plan, especially when you consider the long-term rewards.

Beginning a Routine

If you are a relative newcomer to exercise, we recommend that you start your journey to wellness by joining a gym. First of all, a gym will provide you with exposure to a ton of options. Large gyms give you the choice of free weights, machines, a variety of classes, and possibly a pool. Moreover, you can get professional instruction to help you do the various exercises properly, which is key to avoiding injury.

Speaking of injury, make sure to start slow. You can end up hurt if you take on too much too soon. Moreover, you don't want it to be so hard that you end up quitting. That last part is absolutely critical since your goal is to create a lifelong habit.

Many gyms will provide a complimentary consultation with a trainer for new members. Beyond that, you have the option of hiring a personal trainer. It's an additional expense that may or may not be in the budget, but it's a great way to go if you can swing it. A personal trainer can make sure your technique is good, provide motivation to keep your effort level high, and help you remain accountable to your exercise schedule.

For the long haul, it's important to seek types of exercise that you enjoy (or at least tolerate) rather than ones you hate. Variety is good for the body, so try out many different exercises and keep the ones you like. If there is a particular exercise you really dread, ditch it! Dread is not conducive to a strong habit, and there are so many options that you should never feel locked into any particular style.

••

Finding activities you love

Beyond finding exercises you like or tolerate, the ideal is finding activities that you love that just happen to have the added benefit of exercise. Do you enjoy bike rides, or dancing, or just being outdoors? Any of those can be the basis for a good exercise routine, and an integral part of your overall program.

In fact, even activities like gardening that have you moving around at a low rate of speed can have a positive impact. Multiple studies have shown that too much sitting around can be very hazardous to our health, so any kind of movement beats no movement.[9]

Paraphrasing Newton's First Law of Motion: "A body in motion tends to stay in motion." If you want to keep moving for the long term, keep yourself moving! And what better way to do that than with activities you love?

••

Exercise Essentials

Consistency is the name of the game when it comes to exercise. More than which particular form of exercise you choose, the fact that you exercise *regularly* is what matters. So when choosing workouts, focus on what you can handle (and enjoy) before worrying about what will maximize results.

There are two essential forms of exercise: cardiovascular (aerobic) training and strength (anaerobic) training. Because they offer different benefits, you should incorporate both into your lifestyle. Cardio can help you shave weight and extend your life by keeping your heart and circulatory system in good condition; resistance training is what you need to improve your structure. It keeps you strong, agile and mobile . . . in other words, functionally more youthful. This is something of an oversimplification, but here goes: cardio training helps you live longer, resistance training helps you live better.

Strength (resistance) training can also be helpful in weight-loss efforts. Muscle tissue burns more calories at rest than fat tissue. And your body will continue burning calories at an elevated rate long after a resistance workout is over.[10] Yes, cardio still tends to be king when it comes to losing fat,[11,12] but strength training can aid in that effort while bringing with it a host of other benefits.

A Body in Motion: The importance of cardio

Cardio is the most elemental of workouts . . . walking, running, biking, rowing, swimming, and the like. It's about being on the move, or using fancy equipment that lets you simulate moving while you stay in place.

The term "cardiovascular" refers to the heart and blood vessels, the circulatory system that carries oxygen and nutrients throughout our bodies. Cardiovascular exercise is designed to get that system flowing at an elevated rate for an extended period of time. *Younger Next Year* argues that cardio is important because it emulates the activity of our ancestors who—for most of human existence—had to keep moving in search of food. Not too many of us these days are going to spend much time hunting or foraging for food, but our bodies have evolved for movement; they thrive on it. So it is important that we find a way to work some form of motion into our daily routines.

Now, we realize that fitness levels vary, and for some, you'll literally need to walk before you run (if you ever run at all). Bear in mind that some movement is better than no movement. What is really important is that you incorporate a level of exercise into your daily routine, even if it simply means going for a walk. And if you start slow, hopefully you can ramp up your efforts over time.

A joint report by the American College of Sports Medicine and the American Heart Association suggests older adults adopt one of three options for a cardio routine[13]:

1) Moderate intensity for 30 minutes five days per week

2) Vigorous intensity for 20 minutes three days per week

3) A mix of moderate and vigorous activity three to five days per week

Another approach that has garnered scientific support is high intensity interval (HIIT) training. With HIIT you alternate between short bursts of intense aerobic activity and brief periods of recovery. For example, on a stationary bike, you might pedal like crazy for two minutes, then pedal slowly and catch your breath for one minute. You repeat this cycle again and again over the course of your workout.

Studies suggest that HIIT is superior to traditional exercise programs both in terms of improving your cardiovascular fitness and in terms of fat reduction.[14] Moreover, this approach seems to be better at generating the so called "runner's high" (more on that in a bit), and at building muscle.[15,16] Of course, HIIT probably isn't suitable for beginners, or for those with physical issues that preclude intense workout styles. For more information on the topic, check out this article from AARP that talks about HIIT for seniors: Ultimate Anti-aging Workout.[17]

Lift Things Up and Put Them Down: The importance of strength training

The following summary of a report by Dr. Wayne Westcott of Quincy College paints a pretty compelling picture of the benefits of strength (resistance) training:

> Inactive adults experience a 3% to 8% loss of muscle mass per decade, accompanied by resting metabolic rate reduction and fat accumulation. Ten weeks of resistance training may increase lean weight by 1.4 kg, increase resting metabolic rate by 7%, and reduce fat weight by 1.8 kg. Benefits of resistance training include improved physical performance, movement control, walking speed, functional independence, cognitive abilities, and self-esteem. Resistance training may assist prevention and management of type 2 diabetes by decreasing visceral fat, reducing HbA1c, increasing the density of glucose transporter type 4, and improving insulin sensitivity. Resistance training may enhance cardiovascular health by reducing resting blood pressure, decreasing low-density lipoprotein cholesterol and triglycerides, and increasing high-density lipoprotein cholesterol. Resistance training may promote bone development, with studies showing 1% to 3% increase in bone mineral density. Resistance training may be effective for reducing low back pain and easing discomfort associated with arthritis and fibromyalgia and has been shown to reverse specific aging factors in skeletal muscle.[18]

As if that's not enough, strength training may also reduce the risk of heart disease and depression while improving sleep and helping you live longer.[19,20]

Your muscles, bones, and connective tissues are what enable you to move, and loss of mobility is one of the most devastating impacts of aging. Strength training can be the difference between walking on your own and having to use a wheelchair. Or having your own apartment versus living in a nursing home.

As we age, falling becomes one of the biggest risks we face. Past age 65 one in four of us will fall in any given year.[21] It is the leading cause of fatal injuries and one of the main causes of hospitalization. Improving balance is one of the best of many positive outcomes of exercising in general, and weight training in particular.

Resistance training can be broken down into three primary forms: machines, free weights, and body weight exercises.

- **Machine-based weight training** is most commonly associated with health clubs, where you'll find a plethora of machines, each designed to isolate a certain muscle or group of muscles. The beauty of machines is that they make things somewhat easy. You can follow a circuit of them around the gym and hit all the major muscle groups. The machine guides your motions so that compared with using free weights it's harder to end up using bad form (which can lead to injury). However, the fact that machines guide you is also their biggest drawback.

- **Free weights**—barbells, dumbbells, and kettlebells are the common forms—put the onus entirely on you to guide their motion. Compared to using a machine, you are forced to engage a larger number of supporting muscles in addition to the primary muscle that's being targeted. This leads to well-rounded development of your muscles in a way that is more aligned with activities we encounter in our daily lives. The advantages can be dramatic. One study found that working out with free weights led to a 58% greater increase in strength and a whopping 196% advantage in balance over using machines.[22] That last part might be the most important aspect of lifting weights.

- **Body weight exercises** are one more form worth a mention. Pushups, pull-ups and sit-ups are the most well-known examples, but there are many more. Using the weight of your body for resistance training provides some of the free form benefits of weightlifting, with the added advantage of convenience. If you have a good body weight routine, you carry your gym with you wherever you go.

You certainly don't need to pick just one form of resistance training. A mix of machine, weight, and body weight training is a great way to go. Utilizing a variety of exercises can keep things interesting, will provide a diversity of challenges to your body, and means that when you travel and don't have access to your usual gym/equipment, you will be prepared to improvise.

We again urge you to get some professional guidance when starting an exercise routine. Start with your doctor, and then schedule some time with a fitness trainer. With free weights it is particularly important to develop good form to avoid injury. Whether at a health club or in a home gym, make getting and staying strong part of your game plan.

Body & Mind Exercise

There are a number of forms of exercise that combine physical and mental elements, which is a great combination for seniors. Here are two that we recommend.

Yoga

We've already talked about the risk of falling for seniors. Yoga improves flexibility, strength, and balance and has been shown to reduce the risk of falling.[23] Additional benefits have been found in terms of combatting hypertension, reducing stress, improving sleep patterns and more.[24] There is a meditative aspect to the practice that can be good for mental wellness (more on meditation later).

Many gyms offer a variety of yoga classes. In some communities you'll find dedicated yoga studios offering a range of programs for different types of yoga and varying skill levels. A related form of exercise called Pilates is offered at many yoga studios, and is focused on strength building. Unlike yoga, which utilizes body weight alone, Pilates includes the use of specialized equipment.

Tai Chi

Tai chi is another exercise with roots in Asia that can be beneficial for seniors. A Chinese martial art, tai chi is practiced at a relatively slow rate of movement, making it well-suited for older people who may struggle with mobility and balance. In fact, improved balanced is one of the important benefits of the practice. One analysis of various studies suggests that it may reduce the chance of falls (and related injuries) by 40% or more among older adults and others who are considered at risk for falls.[25]

Studies of tai chi have been somewhat small, so data is limited, but additional potential benefits include relief of pain associated with arthritis, reduced blood pressure, and reduced stress (as with yoga there is a meditative aspect to the practice). Oh, and if you get really good at it, you might even be able to kick some butt—it is, after all, a martial art. We recommend that you keep your expectations in check when it comes to that aspect of tai chi. As best we can tell, most practitioners don't exactly become deadly weapons.

Try searching "tai chi" online for more information; add your zip code to the search to find classes in your area. As with yoga, tai chi has become a thriving exercise subculture with a heavy social element because classes typically take place in groups. See the sidebar for a discussion of another terrific aspect of exercise: the social scene.

. . . .

Exercise as a social activity

We will touch on this a bit more later, but one critical element of happiness and wellness is social connectivity. Many forms of exercise can be done in groups—which could mean you and just one other person (perhaps your spouse or a workout buddy). We know of many couples who run together, for example. Or it can be in large groups such as with yoga, tai chi, or aerobics classes.

There is a natural camaraderie in sharing the struggle of physical exertion, and gyms are great places to chat with friends and meet new people. In fact, having a workout buddy or group is a great way to keep you accountable, and keep you coming back (habit formation). Anything that adds to your enjoyment of exercise gets our seal of approval!

. . . .

The Habit of Good Health

Our attitude is that you should train for retirement like it's the Olympics. Being happy for the rest of your life is a big deal, isn't it? Your odds go way up if you take care of yourself physically and mentally.

It is possible to be a physical mess and still be happy if you wake up every day energized by a sense of purpose (and some people have unavoidable limitations to deal with). But assuming it is achievable for you, think about how much better life is if you are fully mobile, full of energy and vitality, and able to go about your day relatively free of pain. It makes everything else you do easier. Not just easier, but more wonderful. Taking care of yourself doesn't just do your body good, it does your whole being good. Among countless other benefits, exercise has been shown to be an effective treatment for depression, illustrating the connection between mind and body when it comes to wellness.[26]

Exercise—and eating well, as we'll discuss in the next chapter— need to be part of your daily routine, like brushing your teeth. You don't want to have to wake up every day and conduct a debate with yourself about whether or not to exercise. That gets tiresome and is doomed to failure. The goal is to get to the point where you wake up each day and, as Nike says, "Just do it."

What you should try to accomplish is the formation of a habit. Sometimes we think of habits in a negative sense, like drug addiction. But they can be positive as well.

Check out the book *The Power of Habit: Why We Do What We Do in Life and Business*[27] for detailed advice on habit formation. It argues that habits are best created via a combination of triggers and rewards. A trigger might be leaving your workout shoes next to your bed at night so they are the first thing you see in the morning. A reward might be a delicious smoothie or ice coffee with whipped cream after your workout. Or better yet, the reward can simply be feeling great after exercise. In fact, the reward may be partly chemical. Exercise causes the release of endorphins,[28] hormones that stimulate the same receptors in our body that opiates do. Endorphins cause the so-called "runner's high."

Creating a habit is about repetition. One study determined that it takes a minimum of six weeks of working out for four days a week to create a lasting habit.[29] So it is important to seek repetition and consistency. In the beginning, how hard you work out doesn't matter as much as the fact that you do it. You need to build the habit, you need to absorb the activity into your daily routine. Go slow at first, worry about adding intensity later on.

Endnotes

1   Human longevity: Genetics or Lifestyle? It takes two to tango. https://www.ncbi.nlm.nih.gov/pmc/articles/PMC4822264/

2   Lifestyle affects life expectancy more than genetics, Swedish study finds https://www.sciencedaily.com/releases/2011/02/110207112539.htm

3   Social Security Actuarial Life Table. https://www.ssa.gov/oact/STATS/table4c6.html

4   *Younger Next Year: Live Strong, Fit, and Sexy - Until You're 80 and Beyond* by Chris Crowley and Henry S. Lodge (M.D.). ISBN-13: 978-0761147732

5   *The Art and Science of Aging Well: A Physician's Guide to a Healthy Body, Mind, and Spirit* by Mark E. Williams. ISBN-13: 978-1469627397

6   Body-Weight Fluctuations and Outcomes in Coronary Disease http://www.nejm.org/doi/full/10.1056/NEJMoa1606148

7   Defining Adult Overweight and Obesity https://www.cdc.gov/obesity/adult/defining.html

8   Duke-led Study Finds That Moderate-to-Vigorous Workouts Reduce Mortality. https://medicine.duke.edu/medicinenews/duke-led-study-finds-moderate-vigorous-workouts-reduce-mortality

9   What Are the Risks of Sitting Too Much? https://www.mayoclinic.org/healthy-lifestyle/adult-health/expert-answers/sitting/faq-20058005

10   Resistance Exercise: Health Benefits and Medical Applications. http://c.ymcdn.com/sites/members.medicalfitness.org/resource/resmgr/2014_AIC_Presentations_/Wayne_Westcott_presentation.pdf

11   Aerobic Exercise Bests Resistance Training at Burning Belly Fat. https://corporate.dukehealth.org/news-listing/aerobic-exercise-bests-resistance-training-burning-belly-fat

12   Effects of Aerobic and/or Resistance Training on Body Mass and Fat Mass in Overweight or Obese Adults. https://www.physiology.org/doi/10.1152/japplphysiol.01370.2011

13   Physical Activity and Public Health Guidelines: Frequently Asked Questions and Fact Sheet, Physical Activity for the Healthy Adult. https://cph.uiowa.edu/worksafe/pubs/bulletin/Physical-Activity-Healthy-Adults-%20ACSM%20-AHA.pdf

14   High Intensity Training in Obesity: A Meta-analysis. https://www.ncbi.nlm.nih.gov/pmc/articles/PMC5598019/

15   Opioid Release after High-Intensity Interval Training in Healthy Human Subjects. https://www.ncbi.nlm.nih.gov/pubmed/28722022

16   The Effects of High-Intensity Interval Training on Muscle Size and Quality in Overweight and Obese adults. https://www.ncbi.nlm.nih.gov/pubmed/28647284

17   https://www.aarp.org/health/healthy-living/info-2017/anti-aging-workout-fd.html

18   Resistance Training Is Medicine: Effects of Strength Training on Health. https://www.ncbi.nlm.nih.gov/pubmed/22777332

19   The Benefits of Strength Training for Older Adults. https://www.ncbi.nlm.nih.gov/pubmed/14552938

20   Is Strength Training Associated With Mortality Benefits? A 15-year Cohort Study of US Older Adults. https://www.ncbi.nlm.nih.gov/pubmed/26921660

21   Falls Prevention Facts. https://www.ncoa.org/news/resources-for-reporters/get-the-facts/falls-prevention-facts/

22   Strength Outcomes in Fixed Versus Free-Form Resistance Equipment. https://www.ncbi.nlm.nih.gov/pubmed/18296958

23   Yoga's Effect on Falls in Rural, Older Adults. https://www.sciencedirect.com/science/article/pii/S0965229917302698

24   Exploring the Therapeutic Effects of Yoga and Its Ability to Increase Quality of Life. https://www.ncbi.nlm.nih.gov/pmc/articles/PMC3193654/

25   Tai Chi for Risk of Falls: A Meta-analysis. https://www.ncbi.nlm.nih.gov/pubmed/28736853

26   Exercise for the Treatment of Depression and Anxiety.https://www.ncbi.nlm.nih.gov/pubmed/21495519

27   *The Power of Habit: Why We Do What We Do in Life and Business* by Charles Duhigg. ISBN-13: 978-0812981605

28   Endorphins and the Truth About Why Exercise Makes You Happy. https://dailyburn.com/life/fitness/what-are-endorphins-runners-high/

29   Exercise Habit Formation in New Gym Members: A longitudinal study. https://www.cdc.gov/nchs/products/databriefs/db167.htm#ref6

CHAPTER 7

Eating and Thinking Your Way to Better Health

Remember when butter was bad and so were salt, coffee, and cigarettes? (We just wanted to see if you were paying attention! . . . Cigarettes are still bad. See the sidebar if you'd like help quitting.) The scientific consensus on diet has changed over time, so what should you believe? We will explain why diet is such a complicated topic, but we'll also try to isolate some sensible advice within all the noise. We will also talk about the impact that attitude has on health. Wellness is just as much an issue of brain as it is body.

....

Smoking cessation

Smoking lies near the top of the list of things that put your wellness at risk. Not only does it shave a decade or so from your life expectancy, but there are a host of ways it can wreck your quality of life.[1] Of course, smoking is a particularly hard habit to break. If just *knowing* that smoking was harmful was enough to get people to quit, no one would smoke. There is a book called the *Easy Way to Stop Smoking* that some former smokers swear by (it is well-reviewed on Amazon[2]). If you smoke we recommend you give that book a read.

No one approach works for everyone, but you should keep trying until you find what works for you. A number of cessation methods have been found to have some degree of effectiveness, including medication, nicotine replacement therapy, and counseling.[3] Talk to your doctor. Research the subject online. Get it done once and for all.

....

Food for Thought

Food serves a number of sometimes conflicting roles in our lives. First and foremost, food is fuel that we need to survive. But it is also a source of enjoyment, and can be one of life's great pleasures . . . for some, to the point of destructive addiction. Too much food is the cause of some of society's biggest health issues.

So food represents both *need* and *enjoyment*, and then there is a third element: food as a determinant of wellness. That's the complicated part and involves two related factors. First there is nutritional value and the ability for food to promote longevity and help us avoid and fight disease (food as medicine). Second is that poor dietary habits are leading to widespread health issues (food as a source of sickness). Each of us has the power to decide which of those roles food plays in our life—simply by choosing what to eat.

The role of food in determining weight is a national obsession. Annual American spending on weight loss is estimated at $66 billion,[4] and much of that is spent on diet-related products: books, videos, programs, packaged foods, and on and on.

There is reason to believe much of that money is wasted. First, consider that obesity trends have not been improving in the face of all the spending. Americans keep getting fatter and fatter. In fact, since the 1980s the rate of obesity in America has doubled.[5] Even more disturbing, it is up more than threefold among children.

The list of problems associated with obesity is long and scary and includes heart disease, type 2 diabetes, stroke, cancer, and dementia.[6] Belly fat in particular has been found to increase the risk of heart disease, diabetes, and cancer.[7]

Further, there is a correlation between obesity and depression, although it's a bit of a chicken and egg question[8]: does obesity cause depression, or the other way around? It's probably a bit of both.

Beyond the risk of disease, obesity is a lifestyle problem. It's a limiting factor in terms of mobility, energy, and sexual activity.[9] It can mean living with chronic pain, whether from related health issues, or simply from having to carry around extra weight all day.

Figure 7.1: Trends in Obesity Prevalence

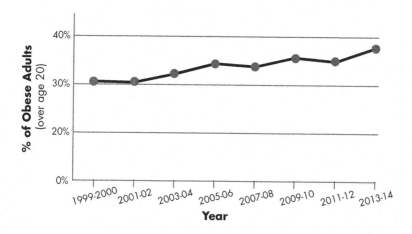

Data for adults aged 20 and older. Source: CDC/NCHS, National Health and Nutrition Examination Study

Eating Healthy

Let food be thy medicine and medicine be thy food.

—*Hippocrates, c. 460-370 BCE*

We mentioned earlier that food is a tougher topic than exercise. Conventional wisdom on diet has gone through so many changes over the years that many people are justifiably confused when it comes to guidance on the subject. Or maybe a better word is "jaded."

For a long time, as depicted in the structure of the famous and now-derided original "food pyramid," it was thought that a healthy diet would be built on a large base of grains like bread, rice, and pasta. Above that, and in increasingly lesser amounts, there were fruits and vegetables, then protein from sources like meats and dairy, and finally at the top, in very small amounts, fat and sugar.

"Heads, fat is bad and carbs are good.
Tails, fat is good and carbs are bad."

Scientific study of the impact of various diets has basically blown the original food pyramid to smithereens—or has at least rearranged it into something very different. Now the thinking goes that vegetables and fruits (in that order) should form the base. Above that we have carbohydrates (bread and pasta, ideally whole grain). Then meat and fish, with dairy sitting above those. Finally, in the smallest amount, sweets (processed sugar) sit at the top of the pyramid.

Figure 7.2: Updated Food Pyramid

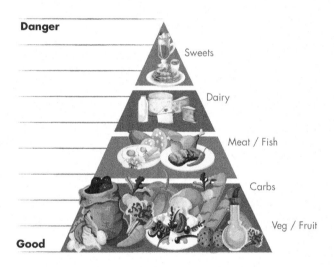

Unfortunately, even the newer version of the pyramid is a subject of debate. Perhaps bread should be in smaller quantities, above meat and fish? And since fruit is full of sugar, should it be somewhat suspect? A hot health topic in recent years has been the difference between good plant-based fat (from avocados and nuts, for example), and bad fats such as those in margarine or meat. None of this is reflected in the pyramid, which seems at best to oversimplify the subject of healthy eating.

It can be hard to get good information about diet because it's such a complex subject. You start with multiple categories like meats, dairy, vegetables, fruits, grains, and nuts. Then within each category there are countless choices. How many vegetables can you think of, for example? Each food carries a mix of different vitamins and minerals. Some of those are critical to our health. But which ones, and in what amounts? Beyond just the variety of foods and the nutrients they carry, there is a variety of food preparations. Food can be processed or whole. It can be raw, grilled, baked, fried, smoked, pickled, or boiled. And preparation sometimes changes the nutrient content.

When it comes to food, the sheer volume of variables can be dizzying. On top of that we are besieged by messages about the latest fad diet that is guaranteed to get us into swimsuit shape in time for summer. Some of those diets even seem to have scientific backing, but amid all the conflicting information . . . who knows?

Yale dietary researcher Dr. David Katz describes the problem like this: "There have been no rigorous, long-term studies comparing contenders for best diet laurels using methodology that precludes bias and confounding. For many reasons, such studies are unlikely."[10] Katz has studied diets extensively, including stars of the day like Paleo and Mediterranean. Thankfully, he seems to have pulled some simple wisdom from all the data and conflicting viewpoints: **"A diet of minimally processed foods close to nature, predominantly plants, is decisively associated with health promotion and disease prevention."**

In fact, when we look at diets that have been found to have scientific support (Mediterranean and Japanese, among others[11,12]), the common denominator seems to be old-school simplicity. What is sold in fancy restaurants as "farm to table," and what your grandmother used to call "breakfast, lunch, and supper," appear to be the cosmic truth of healthy eating. Amidst baffling complexity, it turns out simplicity may be king.

During our research, the theme of minimally processed food with a focus on vegetables came to the fore again and again. In fact, whether the focus was on losing weight, avoiding disease, maintaining fitness, or living longer, the studies mostly pointed in that general direction.

Think Outside the Pyramid

Pop quiz: if you see the following words on a food label, which is most likely to be true health food?

- Low fat

- Low sugar

- Gluten free

- Organic

Trick question! Health food does not come in a box with a label. It's not a packaged meal ready-to-eat, but rather what we might otherwise think of as "ingredients." It is produce (primarily), fish and meat (possibly), natural fats, and spices.

The diet industry shifted from selling packaged goods that were low in fat and high in sugar—which turned out to be totally wrong—to selling packaged goods that are low in carbs, organic, or gluten-free. Those categories can be healthy, but for optimal health don't buy them in processed form. Spinach is low in carbs and gluten-free, and can be organic . . . just buy yourself some spinach!

Focus your food buying in the produce aisle of the supermarket, or to a lesser extent in the butcher section. That's not where you will find "diet" food. There is no diet broccoli, there is just broccoli. Likewise lettuce, apples, and tomatoes.

Learn to prepare and enjoy real fresh food and you will never look back. If you aren't great at it already, why not learn to really cook? It might be the hobby that every retiree should take up.

The web is overflowing with sites and blogs that can guide you to the wonders of healthy whole food cooking. Google "healthy eating advice" or "healthy recipes" and you will be bombarded with options (see Chapter 10 for advice on conducting an effective internet search). Here are a few good resources (others can be found on the Health & Wellness resource page of RetiredHappy.me):

- Nutrition Blog Network—The directory page of this site organizes nutrition-focused blogs into various categories

- LocalHarvest.org—This site helps you locate farmers markets and fresh food throughout the country

- FoodInsight.org—A source for information about healthy eating

- The World's Healthiest Foods—Information and recipes

Check out the book *Food Rules: An Eater's Manual*[13] for a good overview of principles of healthy eating. This and other books on health and wellness can be found on the library page of RetiredHappy.me.

What about alcohol?

There is good news and bad news on this subject. The good news is that data suggests that alcohol in moderation can be good for you.[14] The bad news is that there is a fine line—just one or two drinks—between moderation and too much.

And too much is very bad for you. Aside from the question of the direct health impact from overuse of alcohol, there can be terrible behavioral problems that result from overdrinking. We found conflicting evidence regarding the health impact of moderate use, but above moderate the physical impacts range from bad to deadly. And problems like alcoholism and impaired driving have devastating consequences.

When it comes to alcohol and wellness, remember: you may have seen one of those adorable women on The Today Show celebrating a 102nd birthday, explaining that the secret is a snifter of whiskey every night before bed. But you have never seen a 102-year-old dude who claims the trick is that he crushes a six-pack every afternoon.

Meal delivery services (try searching that phrase for more info)—like Blue Apron and Sun Basket—can make whole-food eating easy. With these subscription-based services you choose to have a certain number of ready-to-cook dinners delivered to your home each week. For each meal you receive a recipe along with the basic ingredients. For example, there might be a whole onion, some peppers, and rice along with a piece of fish and an assortment of spices. The main dish is often accompanied by a salad. Using staples from the pantry (oil, salt and pepper usually) anyone can prepare a delicious fresh meal. You end up enjoying restaurant-quality meals that you might never have imagined otherwise, for a cost of about $10–$13 per person, per meal. Adding a meal delivery service to your weekly repertoire of cooking and dining out can be a great way to add variety to your diet in a healthy way.

Ultimately, choices of food should serve three goals: keep your weight at a healthy level (which ultimately boils down to the overall number of calories you consume), take in enough nutrients to ward off disease (eat a lot of vegetables), and make eating an enjoyable part of your daily routine instead of something that you stress about.

Speaking of stress. ...

Don't Worry, Be Happy (and Healthy)

So far we've talked about physical actions that improve wellness: exercising and eating healthy food. But there is one more step you should take, which may be very easy or very hard depending on your natural disposition. If you are not already, you should try to start looking at things optimistically.

Turns out that optimism is something of a superpower. Being optimistic—assuming that things are likely to turn out for the best— actually correlates to positive health outcomes. One study looked at autobiographies written by nuns when they were in their early twenties.[15] Their writing was evaluated for emotional tone, and those with the most optimistic outlook eventually lived notably longer than the more pessimistic writers.

Many studies have shown an association between having an optimistic worldview and maintaining physical and mental wellness.[16,17,18] Consider the placebo effect, which is the tendency for people to be "fooled" into health benefits when taking something they mistakenly believe to be medicine.[19] The placebo effect is irrefutable evidence of the power of positive thinking.

If you need some guidance on how to embrace optimism in life, check out this little girl—she has a black belt in positive outlook: https://www.youtube.com/watch?v=Cgw8OFVHzd4.

Our title, *Winning in Retirement*, is deliberately upbeat, as is the overall tone of this book. Optimism is powerful. Not only does it feel better than pessimism, but, as we have seen, it can actually drive positive outcomes. That said, millions of American seniors suffer from depression, and the suicide rate is higher among people older than 65 than in any other age group.[20] Whether because of medical depression or due to challenges like illness or personal loss, maintaining a buoyant outlook can be easier said than done.

But you should be mindful of the power of positivity, and you should actively seek it out. At the very least, try not to let the small stuff get you down. Deliberately try to view the glass as half full instead of half empty, and you may discover that perception is reality.

Other Strategies for Mental and Emotional Wellness

Beyond working to develop a positive attitude, pay attention to your overall mental wellness. Do not ignore any mental health issues. While the topic has gained increasing attention in the press, it is still a subject that too many Americans are hesitant to discuss for a variety of reasons. Mental wellness is something you should take as seriously as physical wellness. In fact, the two are very much interrelated. As just one example, there is a chance that much of the increase in depression in our society derives directly from the rise in obesity.[21]

As with all issues related to health, if you are having problems we recommend seeking professional guidance. You can start by talking to your primary care physician, who should be able to direct you to more specialized care as needed. Consider support groups if you are struggling with an issue that is shared by others. Use the web to seek resources. The National Alliance on Mental Illness is one option: https://www.nami.org/Find-Support. But above all, do not ignore a problem, lest it continue or get worse.

One of the most frightening threats facing seniors is that of Alzheimer's and other forms of dementia. Cognitive decline can be devastating, not just for the sufferer but for their loved ones. We stress the need for professional help for such a serious issue, but in our research we have come across some resources we will share related to the topic:

- *The 36-Hour Day* by Nancy L. Mace and Peter V. Rabins is a well-regarded book for families that have to deal with Alzheimer's as caregivers.

- *The Alzheimer's Action Plan* by P. Murali Doraiswamy, M.D., and Lisa P. Gwyther, M.S.W., received plaudits from the Journal of the American Medical Association and other credible sources as a broad look at the subject including prevention, detection, early intervention, and care.

- *The End of Alzheimer's* proposes a process of care that author Dr. Dale Bredesen claims can actually reverse cognitive decline. It seems to be fairly well-reviewed, including by some physicians, although we are not qualified to comment on the validity of the proposed solution.

- See the TED Talk by Lisa Genova for a discussion of what is known about the disease and what might be done to fight it.

TED Talk

Lisa Genova — What you can do to prevent Alzheimer's

Neuroscientist Genova talks about how the disease works, and steps that can be taken to lower your risk.

Aside from dealing with acute issues of mental illness and cognitive decline, there are a variety of practices that can contribute to your mental wellness (and in turn, physical wellness). Here are a few we think are worth your attention:

Meditation—In the book *Tools of Titans*, author Tim Ferriss profiles a number of highly successful individuals, including billionaire entrepreneurs and top performers from the worlds of business, the military, sports, and entertainment. One of the most common themes that emerged from these exceptional individuals is that they meditate. In fact, Ferriss says that 80% of those he interviewed for the book practice meditation of some kind. In addition to anecdotal evidence of meditation being popular among high performers, there is research that suggests the practice can reduce stress and even elicit physical changes.[22] One study found that meditation increases immune response while stimulating the left frontal lobe of the brain.[23] If nothing else, it's relaxing, so give it a try. Apps for your phone like "Headspace" and "Calm" make it easy to learn the practice from the comfort of your couch.

Spirituality—It is certainly not our place to provide specific guidance on a subject as personal as faith. However, we do want to note that generally speaking, having a strong religious or spiritual component to your life has been shown in many studies to have a very positive effect on wellness.[24] Faith, in its many forms, can reduce stress, improve marital outcomes, lessen the likelihood of mental illness, and even improve physical well-being. Also, places of worship can be a critical source of social connection and community support. It is fair to note that religious fervor can have a dark side as well. But having a strong and positive spiritual component to your life can play a key role in wellness, and in your search for happiness (in this world, and perhaps, in the next?).

Charitable efforts—In Chapter 1, we mentioned the correlation between volunteering and living longer, and in Chapter 3 we talked about the idea that giving wealth away might be the best way to gain happiness from it. Turns out this "being a good person" thing can come with fringe benefits.

Social engagement—It seems that feeling lonely or living a life that lacks social engagement (these two things are related but are not necessarily the same) can be very hazardous to your health. It is a risk factor for early death. In fact, being isolated or feeling isolated can be as dangerous as other more well-known risk factors such as obesity, lack of exercise, or substance abuse.[25] Make sure you seek out regular and frequent interactions with other people as part of your happy and healthy retirement lifestyle. (Remember, you can kill two birds with one stone by adding a social aspect to your exercise routines.)

Love—What if we told you there was a special lifestyle element that caused you to be healthier, happier, and live longer? There is, and it's called a happy marriage.[26] Throughout our research we encountered evidence that human connectivity was a big factor in wellness and in happiness, and being married is one of the most significant and impactful forms of connection. Don't go running off to Vegas with just anyone, but do bear in mind that romance can have a powerful beneficial impact on your wellness.

Health and Wellness, Wellness and Health

We have a business partner who is 86 years old. Frank Campbell worked with Pat's dad in the 1980s, and recently joined our business to assure continuity for his clients when he eventually hangs up the spurs. To say that Frank remains professionally and socially active is an understatement.

The mother of one of Pat's best friends is in her 80s (we're not sure of her exact age; it's a heavily guarded secret). Her name is Polly and she is something of a legend. Recently, at a swim meet involving 13 teams, she announced about halfway through that her grandchildren's team was in 5th place . . . she had been keeping score during the endless series of relay and individual races. Sharp? To say the least. In her 60s, Polly used to get in trouble for scaling the fence at the swim club to do laps before the crack of dawn. Currently she either swims 50 laps or walks five miles per day. There is no question that she has the life she leads today—independent and immersed in the lives of her children and grandchildren—because wellness is a big part of her life. She made it a habit long ago; it would be unthinkable for her to not exercise (both physically and mentally).

Wellness is a vast topic that we could never adequately cover in one book, much less two chapters of a book. So as with other subjects related to finding happiness in retirement, our goal has been to provide a basic framework that should help you lay out your game plan. (In the final chapter we will pull it all together.)

Most of all, we hope we've made it clear that much of wellness is self-reinforcing: happiness leads to better health and better health leads to greater happiness. Exercise and eating well makes us more energetic, which encourages us to be more active. Feeling good about yourself makes you more likely to take of yourself, which makes you feel better. It is up to you to put these virtuous cycles in motion and keep them going by forming positive habits.

As discussed in the previous chapter, make exercise part of your daily routine if it isn't already. Start exercising every day in some form or another, until it becomes so ingrained in your life that you can't imagine doing without it. Seek the joy, the buzz, and the lifelong rewards that physical activity can provide. At the same time, build your diet around whole foods. Let food be your medicine by eating ample amounts of fresh fruits and, especially, vegetables. And don't ignore your mental wellness. Be active socially, read, learn, stretch your brain.

Among all the actions you can take to increase your chances of happiness in retirement, this is the most obvious of the bunch: take good care of yourself. And while you're at it, try to look at the world through rose-colored glasses, because having a positive attitude can help make good things happen.

Endnotes

1   Tobacco-Related Mortality. https://www.cdc.gov/tobacco/data_statistics/fact_sheets/health_effects/tobacco_related_mortality/index.htm

2   Easy Way to Stop Smoking. https://www.amazon.com/dp/B01EVMK0H0/ref=dp-kindle-redirect?_encoding=UTF8&btkr=1

3   5 Smoking Cessation Studies Every Pharmacist Should Know. http://www.pharmacytimes.com/contributor/timothy-o-shea/2017/06/5-smoking-cessation-studies-every-pharmacist-should-know

4   U.S. Weight Loss Market Worth $66 Billion. https://www.prnewswire.com/news-releases/us-weight-loss-market-worth-66-billion-300573968.html

5   Obesity Rates & Trends Overview. https://stateofobesity.org/obesity-rates-trends-overview/

6   The Health Effects of Overweight and Obesity. https://www.cdc.gov/healthy-weight/effects/index.html

7   Fibroblast growth factor receptor is a mechanistic link between visceral adiposity and cancer. https://www.nature.com/articles/onc2017278?foxtrot-callback=true

8   Depression and Obesity in the U.S. Adult Household Population, 2005–2010. https://www.ncbi.nlm.nih.gov/pubmed/25321386

9   Sexuality and Obesity, a Gender Perspective: Results from French National Random Probability Survey of Sexual Behaviours. https://www.bmj.com/content/340/bmj.c2573

10 Katz's comments are excerpted from an article in The Atlantic. https://www.theatlantic.com/health/archive/2014/03/science-compared-every-diet-and-the-winner-is-real-food/284595/

11 Mediterranean Diet and Prevention of Coronary Heart Disease in the Elderly. https://www.ncbi.nlm.nih.gov/pmc/articles/PMC2684076/

12 Soy and Fish as Features of the Japanese Diet and Cardiovascular Disease Risks. https://www.ncbi.nlm.nih.gov/pmc/articles/PMC5400241/

13 *Food Rules: An Eater's Manual* by Michael Pollan. ISBN-13: 978-0143116387

14 Alcohol: If You Drink It, Keep It Moderate. https://www.mayoclinic.org/healthy-lifestyle/nutrition-and-healthy-eating/in-depth/alcohol/art-20044551

15 Positive Emotions in Early Life and Longevity: Findings from the Nun Study. https://www.ncbi.nlm.nih.gov/pubmed/11374751

16 Optimism and Its Impact on Mental and Physical Well-Being. https://www.ncbi.nlm.nih.gov/pmc/articles/PMC2894461/

17 The Immune System and Happiness. http://www.ncbi.nlm.nih.gov/pubmed/17027886

18 Happiness and Life Satisfaction Prospectively Predict Self-rated Health, Physical Health, and the Presence of Limiting, Long-term Health Conditions. https://www.ncbi.nlm.nih.gov/pubmed/18785370

19 The Power of the Placebo Effect. https://www.health.harvard.edu/mental-health/the-power-of-the-placebo-effect

20 The Five Most Taboo Topics In Retirement: #5 Mental Health. https://www.forbes.com/sites/robertlaura/2017/11/29/the-five-most-taboo-topics-in-retirement-5-mental-health/#79533ce91b5f

21 Depression Prevalence: Is it Really Increasing? https://www.ncbi.nlm.nih.gov/pubmed/18612864

22 University of Wisconsin Study Reports Sustained Changes In Brain And Immune Function After Meditation. http://www.sciencedaily.com/releases/2003/02/030204074125.htm

23 Alterations in Brain and Immune Function Produced by Mindfulness Meditation. https://www.ncbi.nlm.nih.gov/pubmed/12883106

24 Religion, Spirituality, and Health: The Research and Clinical Implications https://www.ncbi.nlm.nih.gov/pmc/articles/PMC3671693/

25 Loneliness and Social Isolation as Risk Factors for Mortality: A Meta-Analytic Review. https://www.ahsw.org.uk/userfiles/Research/Perspectives%20on%20Psychological%20Science-2015-Holt-Lunstad-227-37.pdf

26 The Effects of Marriage on Health: A Synthesis of Recent Research Evidence. https://aspe.hhs.gov/pdf-report/effects-marriage-health-synthesis-recent-research-evidence

CHAPTER 8

Your Legacy

"To live in hearts we leave behind is not to die."

—Thomas Campbell

Afriend of ours told us about a conversation she had with her then 80-year-old mother, who was still living in the family's home of 50 years.

"Mom," said our friend, "would you like some help cleaning out all those boxes in the attic?"

"No," came the reply. "I'm going to leave it to you and your sister to sort out."

Many relatives have faced situations like this when it comes to dealing with a lifetime's worth of possessions. Unfortunately, it's also an all-too-common tactic that people use with regard to their investments and other assets. They fail to document their preferences and instead leave it to "others" (which can include the government!) to decide who gets what. Is that how you want your legacy to be decided?

Let's face it—sooner or later, all efforts at health and wellness will come to naught, and we will pass into the great beyond. It's not an easy subject, but it's an important one. Especially from the perspective of the loved ones you leave behind.

In this chapter, we will explain some basic concepts of estate planning, and describe common pitfalls that can leave families in disarray absent proper planning. Our intent is not to dive into the endless details of trusts or tax law: the rules are very complex and subject to change. In fact, if another election has happened by the time you are reading this, the laws may already be quite different from what they were while we were writing this.

The good news is that with a bit off effort, and perhaps a small outlay of legal fees, you can do an incredible amount of good for your family—and, if you are charitably inclined, for humanity.

....

Legal help

Estate planning is complex enough that you should have professional legal help with it. Yes, you can handle some of the decisions and paperwork on your own, but the laws vary a lot from state to state and it's not always clear to a layperson how to word their wishes and instructions in a way that conforms to legal statutes.

We recommend you work with a lawyer who specializes in estate planning, no matter whether you have a very simple estate and just want a will, or if your situation requires more complex documents and instructions. You should be able to tell by looking them up online if an attorney specializes in estate planning. They should list estate planning as their primary focus, not just one of many services they offer.

Any lawyer can draw up wills and trusts, but working with a specialist helps ensure that you will be in the hands of someone who knows that area of law very well. In seeking a qualified attorney (as with seeking any qualified professional), you can begin by asking around to friends, family, and trusted advisors.

....

It's common to dread the subject of estate planning, as it involves facing our own mortality. As a result, most people put it off or ignore it altogether. However, you can gain great satisfaction by getting your affairs in order, especially when it means you have taken care of the people who mean the most to you. There is one simple theme we will stress on this subject, borrowed from the Boy Scouts: be prepared.

Estate Planning Goals

The need for estate planning boils down to a handful of goals. First among them is the ability to dictate what happens to your accumulation of money and belongings (your "estate") after you die. If you don't make the decisions, then the relevant laws in your state will, and you may not be happy with the results, as we'll discuss below.

The decisions you make in estate planning include who you want to benefit—usually family and/or charities—and who you do *not* want to benefit. You can also describe how you want any benefits to be transferred. For example, maybe rather than providing a bequest to a child immediately, you might prefer to pay it out over time, or make it contingent on achieving certain life goals.

Another aim of estate planning, particularly for the very wealthy, is avoidance of taxes. If you have a lot of money and you want most of it to go to your heirs or to charity instead of to the government, it will require planning.

Lastly, the use of trusts can shelter your money from lawsuits, or from losses that might result from marriages that fall apart (whether yours or your heirs').

Estate Planning Tools

Estate planning is accomplished through the use of legal documents, including:

1) Wills

2) Trusts

3) Beneficiary designations

Wills

A will is the document that most of us think about when it comes to distributing assets at death. It is a set of instructions that are provided to a court when you pass, explaining what you would like to happen to your things after you are gone.

If you die "intestate" (without a will), the court will decide what happens to your stuff, using a prescribed set of rules. According to a Gallup survey, only about 44% of Americans have a will.[1] The problem with dying without a will is that the rules for estate distribution might not match your wishes at all. The rules vary depending on where you live, but here are some examples based on the Uniform Probate Code that forms the basis of many State laws:

- If you are married and die with children that you had together, your spouse inherits everything.

- If you are married and die without children, but your parents are alive, your spouse gets the first $200,000, and the remainder is split 75% to your spouse and 25% to your parents.

- If you are married and you each have children from previous marriages, your spouse gets the first $150,000, and the remainder is split 50% to your spouse and 50% among the children.

As you can see, the rules can seem somewhat arbitrary. Do not settle for arbitrary! At the very least you should draft a will. Presumably, many people put off drafting a will in part because they do not want to face the concept of death, and in part because the costs can be high.

While we generally recommend working with an estate planning attorney, it is possible to create your own will for very low cost using online services (such as BuildaWill.com or Legalzoom.com), or by purchasing standard forms at an office supply store.

If your estate is somewhat complex—either by virtue of a complicated family structure or because of the amount of wealth involved—we urge you to get legal help. But any will is better than no will at all. You do not want your last act on this earth to be leaving behind a mess for your family to deal with.

Beneficiary Designations

A will is not the only way to dictate where your assets go upon death. Some investments (annuities, for example) and retirement accounts (such as IRAs and 401(k)s), allow for **beneficiary designations** that say who is to inherit the money. A beneficiary designation allows your heirs to bypass the will/probate process. When you pass away, those accounts immediately belong to the loved one or charity of your choice. In the case of a spouse, they can roll the proceeds of your IRA directly into their own retirement account (with no tax consequences).

It works a little bit differently when you leave a retirement account to your children or to anyone other than your spouse. In that case, the beneficiary has the option of taking the money right away (it will be taxable to them as income, except in the case of Roth accounts), or rolling the money into an inherited IRA. With an inherited IRA, your heir can spread the distributions (and the tax consequences) over their life expectancy. The long-run financial impact can be considerable.

If you fail to designate a beneficiary for an IRA, it becomes part of your estate when you pass away, and the distribution of the proceeds will be dictated by your will. In that case, the money has to come out of the IRA (and be taxed) within five years. This is a less-than-ideal outcome that can be avoided simply by making sure you have filled out a beneficiary designation form (ask your retirement plan provider for help with this).

Trusts

A trust is another legal structure that can be helpful in estate planning. It's a complicated subject we will not cover in great detail, but we want you to understand the basic concepts so you can decide if some kind of trust might be helpful for you and your family.

There are two primary categories of trusts: revocable and irrevocable. Each is intended to achieve different goals.

A **revocable trust** (the name indicates that you can change it at any time) is essentially a replacement for a will. Like a beneficiary designation, a revocable trust directs your assets to beneficiaries immediately upon your death. When you die, the trust essentially ceases to exist and your assets immediately belong to your heirs—and the portion of your estate covered by the trust does not need to go through the probate (court) system. The cost and complexity of the probate system varies from state to state, but no matter where you are, avoiding it can be a nice thing for your heirs. Also, anything that goes through probate court becomes part of the public record. So if you value your privacy and don't want anyone to be able to peer into your personal business (which becomes your heirs' personal business) after your death, using a trust is preferable.

An **irrevocable trust** is an entirely different kind of animal. With an irrevocable trust you permanently give away assets. They cease to belong to you, and instead belong to a vehicle you have created that is set up to carry out your wishes. While a revocable trust ends with your death (or the death of you and your spouse), and the resulting distribution of assets, an irrevocable trust can live on indefinitely. There are several possible upsides to this sort of trust:

- **Potential tax benefits:** When assets are placed into an irrevocable trust, they cease to be part of your estate, which can have tax benefits if you have enough money to be subject to estate taxes. Each person has an estate tax exemption, which is the amount you can give away either during your life or at death, of $11,200,000 ($22,400,000 per couple) as of the time of this writing. So at the moment, avoiding such taxes is a concern only for people with a lot of money. That could easily change in the future, though, as estate tax rules are something of a political football. In fact, if we had to lay odds, we'd bet on the estate exemption coming down at some point, maybe way down.

- **Longevity of care for your family/heirs.** If you die or otherwise become unable to handle your affairs, a trust can carry out your wishes long after you are gone, including looking after your family. If you have minor children, an irrevocable trust can provide structured financial support until they reach adulthood. For older children you can base their inheritances on the achievement of goals, such as college graduation or reaching a certain age. Or you can make sure that not only do your children receive support, but their children as well. You can also set up gifts to charities that can keep having an impact for a very long time (forever, in some cases).

- **Avoiding unintended lousy consequences.** For example, imagine you pass away and your spouse remarries. Absent a trust, if your spouse then passes away, whoever they married could end up with all of your money while your children get nothing or very little! The same kinds of issues can arise if you get divorced.

- **Providing you and your family with legal protections.** Let's say you—or one of your family members after you pass—is involved in an accident, or someone slips and falls on the sidewalk in front of your house. You can be sued for everything you own, but it would be much harder for someone to successfully sue for money in an irrevocable trust (because those assets technically no longer belong to you).

Communication

There are two common repercussions when a spouse or other family member passes way. The first, of course, is grief. The second is chaos. The chaos can be largely avoided with a bit of planning.

Much of the confusion and difficulty that ensues upon the passing of a loved one can be avoided through communication. Do you want to be buried or cremated? Do you know what kind of service you would like, and where it should be held? You should communicate these things to those who are closest to you. You should also let them know where your will and other important documents can be found (more on this in a minute).

In short, do not leave your loved ones with a mess to sort out in their time of grief. They are going to be dealing with a lot as it is. You should avoid saddling them with confusion and easily avoided stress on top of it all. Again, we realize this is not an easy subject. It's not something that you, or for that matter your spouse and kids (if applicable), are going to enjoy discussing. But a little discussion in advance goes a very long way toward making things easier for them when the time comes.

Informal discussions of your wishes can be as helpful as the legal preparations (wills and trusts) that we discussed earlier. But appropriate documentation is important as well. Many families are torn to shreds by battles that ensue because of disagreements over what should happen after someone passes. Fights over money are not uncommon, but there can also be fights over funeral plans, where to hold a wake, or who gets your prized Beanie Babies collection. Remember, emotions will be running high, and it's easy for those emotions to turn to strife. Do you want your legacy to be a family in angry disarray?

The key to avoiding that kind of mess is to clearly express what your wishes are, via discussion, legal documentation, and the tool we will discuss next.

The Family Organizer

There is a simple and powerful way to make sure your affairs are in order in the event you become incapacitated or pass away. We call it the **"family organizer."** It's a binder that summarizes important personal and financial information. What could be easier than that?

Everything you need for a family organizer can be found at an office supply store. You'll want a three-ring binder and a pack of pocket sleeves. If you really want to get fancy, you can print out labels for each of the sleeves.

When we create a family organizer for clients, we have a sleeve for each of the following categories:

- Personal info guide—this is a summary of everything. You list assets and liabilities, and every account that your spouse or kids need to know about. We have a downloadable version on RetiredHappy.me. You should include usernames for your online accounts. For safety's sake do not list passwords, but consider using a password known by the family. Otherwise, at least make sure that your spouse knows the password for your email accounts; that way he or she can use the password recovery tool to get into your accounts.

- Income tax returns—keep two year's worth

- Bank statements—a years' worth is probably sufficient

- Investment statements

- Mortgage statements

- Loan statements

- Life insurance policies

- Employee benefit information (especially anything about life insurance, or portable policies for benefits such as long-term care)

- Social Security statements

- Wills/trusts (these may be too large to fit in a binder sleeve, but keep them in the same place as the binder)

- Miscellaneous

Of course, make sure that your loved ones know of the existence of the binder and where it is stored. Imagine if, upon your passing, instead of having to figure things out for themselves and search all over creation for paperwork and information, they could simply open a binder and everything they needed would be at their fingertips. That is a true gift of love.

What Will Be Your Lasting Impression?

If you've ever had to deal with the estate of someone who was not organized and did not have the right documents in place, you know how time consuming and difficult it is for those left behind. Dealing with courts and government agencies is no fun for anyone. So if for no other reason than to save your family a lot of hassle, do some basic estate planning. As we said at the beginning of this chapter, a little effort goes a long way when it comes to looking after your affairs. Do not be one of the majority of people who procrastinate on this stuff!

You are going to pass away at some point. And if you are a man, you are probably going to do so before your wife does. Do something about it.

Don't let your reluctance to face up to mortality, or a general tendency to procrastination, result in a mess for your family. The last great gift you can give them is to leave this world with your affairs in order, and it's really not that difficult. Create a will, create a binder. Maybe plan your funeral as well. It's that simple, and it is so important.

Endnotes

1   Majority In U.S. Do Not Have a Will. http://news.gallup.com/poll/191651/majority-not.aspx

CHAPTER 9

Location, Location, Location

You are now free to move about the country.

Southwest Airlines commercial

A ctually, you are now free to move about the world (within reason). This is a fun chapter where you get to relax and fantasize about some amazing places to live. Actually, "fantasize" is the wrong word; better to call it "planning." By now you should be thinking about retirement as an opportunity for reinvention. That includes the possibility of relocating to somewhere new and exciting.

"Where to live?" is a broad question that goes beyond geography to include subjects like lifestyle, family, practicality, and finances. Do you want to live someplace warm? Do you want to wake up every morning to a beautiful view? Or is living near children and grandchildren a priority? Do you think living in a retirement community sounds appealing, or do you hate that idea?

Deciding where to live is a very personal choice. There are a number of common factors to consider, and ultimately your decision will be based on how much weight you give to each of them.

The book *America's 100 Best Places to Retire*—a great source for information and inspiration—rates locations based on the following criteria:

Population

- Location
- Climate
- Cost of living
- Housing cost
- Religion

- Education
- Transportation
- Walk Score
- Healthcare
- Taxes[22]

We are not going to touch on all of these topics, but we will hit some highlights and also talk about various housing and financing options. Initially we will focus on retiring within the United States,

"And they lived happily ever after until they received the property tax bill for their castle."

although the same ideas apply to retiring abroad, an option we will address later.

Your Ideal Scenario

There are many practical considerations when it comes to choosing where to live in retirement. Most people have to work within a budget, and some have health issues to consider, or want or need to remain near family. But before you get too bogged down by constraints, we recommend that you take some time to imagine your theoretical ideal.

For example, where we live, some people maintain two houses in retirement. These so-called "snow birds" live in the Northeast (near family) during spring and summer, and migrate South (often to Florida) during the colder months. In addition to climate advantages, living in Florida for more than six months of the year can have notable tax advantages (more on that subject later).

With enough money, it's possible to have your cake and eat it too when it comes to retirement living. A house near your kids, and a house at the beach? A house in the mountains, and an apartment in the city? As the philosopher Ferris Bueller once said: "If you have the means, I highly recommend it."

Maybe you have no interest in maintaining more than one home. Is your ideal situation to live in a community with resort-like amenities and healthcare services that you can use for the rest of your life? Or to downsize to a one-story bungalow that will be easy to care for?

Here are some common retirement-living scenarios:

1. Stay where you are now

2. Keep two (or more) residences indefinitely

3. Move from one place to another at retirement

4. Keep two homes for a while, with the aim of consolidating to one later in retirement

The idea is to come up with an attainable dream scenario, and then plan to make that scenario—or something close to it—real. During the rest of this chapter we'll present some factors that can help you make a choice that is right for you. In the final chapter, recording your preferences will be part of the action steps we will guide you through.

Geography

When someone asks "Where do you want to live in retirement?" they are typically referring to geographic location. What state (or country) do you want to live in? Do you prefer city or rural living? In making such choices, there are a number of factors that are important to retirees. Here's a quick review of some of the most important considerations.

Healthcare

The availability of quality medical care varies from place to place. Generally speaking, the best care can be found around big cities, where top hospitals and their related healthcare systems are located. Care tends to be best in the Northeast and Midwest, and weakest in the South.[1] Typically, the more affluent an area is, the better the healthcare.

This is of particular importance if you or your spouse has a medical condition that requires special care. There is a wealth of information available on this topic via the internet, including a number of state-by-state rankings.[2]

Bear in mind that the world of healthcare is very much in flux. No one knows what healthcare in America will look like in the future. Depending on the way the political squabbles play out, the cost disparity between states could shrink or grow. We will keep updated information available on the Health & Wellness page of RetiredHappy.me.

Taxes

Perhaps even more so than with healthcare, stark differences exist between the states when it comes to taxation. Some states tax income, others do not. Some tax estates (the money you pass along to your heirs), some do not. Property taxes are another subject of great variability. The differences, particularly if you have managed to amass considerable wealth or if you expect to have a high income in retirement, can be significant.

Although regional tax rules are not experiencing the sort of seismic shift we see in the world of healthcare, laws do change from time to time. You should pay attention to the political climate in an area in addition to the current tax rules as you weigh the financial desirability of a state or town as a retirement destination.

There are tax resources available on the internet, including the following two web pages that include interactive maps: Retirement Living—Taxes by State,[3] and Kiplinger's State-by-State Guide to Taxes on Retirees.[4]

Climate and the Outdoors

Do you enjoy experiencing the changing of the seasons, or would you prefer to leave the cold behind for good? Are you a golfer, a skier,[5] or a hiker?

Our nation is blessed with an incredible variety of climates and topographies. Have you seen the beautiful mountains and deserts of New Mexico . . . every sunset is a work of art in Santa Fe! Want to stroll the beaches of Florida for the rest of your life? How about California wine country, or the redwoods? Is lakeside living more your style?

Think of the greatest vacation you ever had, and then think about the fact that you can live in a place like that. What's to stop you? Well, more on that next.

Proximity to Family

Perhaps the biggest limiting factor when it comes to choosing a retirement destination is the desire to be near your children, grandchildren, or other family members. For many, there can be no greater joy, beaches be damned!

Not only is this desire perfectly understandable, but it can be practical as well. As we get deeper into retirement, the support of family may become medically or financially necessary. Moreover, proximity to family may be the thing you value most of all.

One option is to live as close to family as possible. For some, this may mean living on the same property or in the same home. Another approach to consider is what we call the "family magnet factor," which means living somewhere that family will want to go. We see this with retirees who live in Florida or California or some other attractive, vacation-friendly spot. A "destination" home your children and grandchildren love to visit can be a great option short of actually living in the same town. Not only do you get to live in a wonderful spot, but your home acts as a magnet that helps draw family to you. In this case, consideration has to be given to the size of your home, since you will need something big enough to allow you to play host on a regular basis.

Earlier we talked about the development of automated driving technology. Think of the potential impact when it comes to retirement location. A seven-hour drive might be arduous now, but it will be less so if the car is handling most or all of the driving. In the same way that passenger airlines made the world smaller and more accessible, automated driving could represent a travel revolution. Bear that in mind when you consider what "too far" is when it comes to proximity to family. At the time of this writing, driverless cabs were being tested in America. The technology will be here sooner than you might expect.

City vs. Country

There is a fundamental lifestyle difference between living in the city and living in the suburbs or a rural area. The physical environment, entertainment and dining options, taxation, social scenes, and shopping options are different.

For many there is a strong preference for one or the other. Some people are clearly country folk, some city folk. If you spent a lifetime living in one or the other the idea of switching may seem as outlandish as moving to a foreign country (more on that idea in a bit). But for those who appreciate both styles of living, a decision may need to be made, and there are a number of variables to consider.

Usually you can find better levels of medical care in and around urban centers. In fact, there is a growing gap in life expectancy between people who live in cities and those who live in rural areas.[6] Much of that gap can be explained by issues that you can personally control for, such as higher rates of smoking and obesity in rural areas. But accidents are also more common in rural areas, and, as we said, access to quality healthcare is typically lower.

Big cities offer a broader selection of restaurants, museums, theaters and other forms of entertainment. Cities also offer a lifestyle that is conducive to walking as a mode of transportation, which is a great way to keep your health up. You can walk to dinner, walk to visit friends, walk to grab your coffee in the morning, even walk to get your groceries.

Check out this New York Times article[7] for an interesting perspective on the importance of walking, and how the goal of being more walkable is shaping communities across the country. The website walkscore.com ranks the walkability of cities and neighborhoods in America (as well as Canada and Australia). Ratings are on a scale from 1 to 100, with low-rated areas described as "Car Dependent" and high-rated areas as "Walker's Paradise." The site also provides a Bike Score and a Transit Score. You can check the Walk Score for a particular town on the Location page of RetiredHappy.me.

Some people who choose to live in big cities forgo car ownership altogether to avoid high parking fees and other costs of car ownership. For those without a car, having a good variety of transportation options

own borders there is a tremendous diversity of places to live and visit. Beyond that, there are cultural and financial considerations that tend to keep Americans close to home.

That said, many Americans do choose to live abroad. The U.S. does not keep formal track, but in 1999 the State Department estimated the number at between 3 and 6 million.[14] If you do consider moving or keeping a second home abroad, you open up a very wide spectrum of enticing lifestyles to choose from.

Most of the same considerations that go into determining where to live domestically apply to overseas living, albeit with additional tax and legal wrinkles to consider. There is certainly more of a learning curve involved, unless you are already very familiar with the foreign destination you're considering.

A great resource on this topic is *How to Retire Overseas: Everything You Need to Know to Live Well (for Less) Abroad.*[15] The book breaks things down to the following points of evaluation:

- Cost of living
- Cost of housing (buying or renting)
- Climate
- Healthcare
- Infrastructure
- Easy access to and from the United States
- Culture
- Recreation and entertainment
- Taxes
- Special benefits for foreign retirees
- Education and schools (if you are moving with children)
- Safety

An additional question, which touches on many of the above, is whether you plan to immerse yourself in the local culture and live among the natives, or if you plan to live in a community of English-speaking expats. The latter may be the easier route, but it may be more expensive and it could take away from the experience you seek.

Wherever you might live abroad, seek out local tax and legal representation. If you have a medical condition or lifestyle that puts you at high risk of accident or injury, you also need to pay special attention to the availability of quality healthcare.

In describing the decision to move abroad, *How to Retire Overseas* very aptly says: "More than a country, you're choosing a way of life." If living outside the United States is something you would like to consider, we recommend that book as a starting point for your research. It contains much more detail on the subjects referenced here, including recommendations for certain countries that tend to be hospitable for retiring Americans.

Additional resources to check out include *Retirement Without Borders*[16] by Barry Golson (although, since the book was written in 2008, the information may be a bit dated), and the website www.Internationalliving.com. The internet can provide a wealth of tips to help guide you, although be aware that much of the information you'll encounter will come from businesses trying to sell you something. In fact, that's a common issue when it comes to researching on the web, a subject we'll cover in the next chapter.

Retirement Communities

Beyond the options of renting vs. buying, and homes vs. apartments, most people will at some point consider living in some sort of retirement community. The three primary types are:

1) **Independent living communities**—for healthy, active seniors who are seeking a community that provides social options as well as amenities such as gyms, pools, housekeeping and transportation. They can be individual homes, apartments, or condos. There may be purchase or rental options, and costs vary widely based on the quality of the accommodations.

2) **Assisted living communities**—for seniors who remain somewhat independent but require assistance with activities like dressing, bathing, taking medication or eating. These are usually condos or apartments. Typically, meals are provided in a common dining area, and staff is available to help in an emergency 24 hours a day. According to the 2017 Genworth Financial Cost of Care Survey,[17] the national median monthly cost for an assisted living facility in 2017 was $3,750. But it varies by region (and, of course, by quality of facility). Check out this link[18] to research median costs in various states.

3) **Nursing homes**—for people who are unable to care for themselves and who need medical assistance (short of hospital care). Nursing home care is very expensive, averaging $7,148 a month for a semi-private room and $8,121 for a private room (per the Genworth survey). There are also Special Care Units for dementia and Alzheimer's patients.

An option that covers all these bases is a Continuing Care Retirement Community (CCRC). In a CCRC you start out with an independent living lifestyle, and then progress into higher levels of care as needed. In other words you may live in your own townhome early in retirement, but in a nursing home later on . . . all within the same community.

While the idea of a retirement community may seem almost painfully practical, in reality some of them are so well-appointed and come with such nice amenities that they inspire comparison to cruise ships. Plus, they offer ample opportunities to remain socially engaged, which, as we have seen, is a critical factor in terms of wellness and happiness.

As mentioned earlier, one of the members of our team, Frank Campbell, is 86 years old at the time of this writing. Frank is a model of living life to the fullest later in life. He has no financial need to work, but continues to do so because it keeps him engaged and because he loves working with his clients. He is physically fit, and remains extremely active socially. We visited Frank at a retirement community where he and some of our clients live (they are close friends of Frank as well as clients), and came away with a different perspective on what it means to live in a place like that.

First of all, the social network in the community is very strong. It has a country club feel to it, everybody knows everybody else, and there is never a lack of things to do. Moreover, Frank and both of the lady clients who live there are widowed, as are many other members of the community. Frank and his friends had all moved into the community with spouses, but lost them at some point along the way. As one of them put it, when someone experiences a loss, "the community wraps its arms around you." That's a profound concept, and one worth considering as you ponder where you want to be in the future.

Moreover, Frank and his friends rave about the quality of medical assistance available to those who need it. They have a terrific person on staff who is able to provide guidance about health issues (she helped us with the Medicare chapter), and in-home care is provided as needed.

This comprehensive "best of all worlds" approach has great appeal, but it typically comes with a hefty price tag to match. According to AARP you can expect to pay between $100,000 and $1 million upfront for the typical CCRC, in addition to monthly charges of $3,000–$5,000 (maybe more as needs increase).[19]

Check out https://www.medicare.gov/nursinghomecompare/search.html for a listing of retirement facilities including ratings for health inspections, staffing, and overall quality. You might also look into the Long-Term Care Ombudsman Program.[20] Every state is required to offer these advocacy groups that help individuals with issues related to quality of care.

Renting Out Your Home

Of course, with enough money you can have houses wherever you want. But it is possible to be "multi-locational" without having accumulated a huge amount of wealth. For example, you could rent out either your secondary or your primary home (or both) when not in use, as a way to generate extra income and cover housing expenses.

Just as Uber and Lyft have revolutionized the business of calling for a car, services like Airbnb and VRBO have created a new, relatively easy way of renting out property. You list your home as available during a particular period at a particular price, and renters are easily able to find it. The technology simplifies the transaction, and a rating system helps weed out lousy renters (and lousy homes).

You can exchange keys with a renter in person, or utilize a lockbox, coded door lock, or key exchange company to avoid in-person contact. Check out the site Learnairbnb.com for an overview of these and other details about how the service works, or Google "how does Airbnb work" to find a number of articles on the subject. For a deeper dive (with an emphasis on maximizing the financial results of renting), check out the book *Get Paid for Your Pad: How to Maximize Profit From Your Airbnb Listing.*[21]

Of course, the idea of renting your home to strangers may be off-putting, and there have been instances of crime and property damage resulting from such transactions. But if you are comfortable with the idea and do your homework, the "sharing economy" could open up a new realm of income and living options for you.

The reverse is true as well. Consider home rental websites as an option for vacations. It is possible to rent fabulous homes throughout the world for the same or even lower costs than a hotel room.

Adventurer or Homebody?

One of the most exciting aspects of retirement is that you might choose to live somewhere new. There are issues of family and practicality that may impose some limits, but you should dare to dream when it comes to location. We will revisit this subject when we talk about modern retirement tools, and again when we define the steps for planning your happy retirement. Few decisions are as important as where to live when it comes to shaping what the rest of your life is going to look like.

"My real estate agent found me this place. I said I wanted a home that requires no yard work, no painting, no snow shoveling. A place where the weather is perfect and neighbors never complain about my music..."

Endnotes

1   Health Care Rankings. https://www.usnews.com/news/best-states/rankings/health-care

2   Best & Worst States for Health Care. https://wallethub.com/edu/states-with-best-health-care/23457/

3   https://www.retirementliving.com/taxes-by-state

4   http://www.kiplinger.com/tool/retirement/T055-S001-state-by-state-guide-to-taxes-on-retirees/index.php

5   See 70plusskiclub.org for an organization dedicated to senior skiers

6   Gap in Life Expectancy Between Rural and Urban Residents Is Growing. http://www.cfah.org/hbns/2014/gap-in-life-expectancy-between-rural-and-urban-residents-is-growing

7   https://www.nytimes.com/2016/10/15/business/
    the-future-of-retirement-communities-walkable-and-urban.
    html?rref=collection%2Fsectioncollection%2Fhealth&action=click&contentCol-
    lection=health&region=stream

8   The New Real Estate Mantra: Location Near Public Transportation. https://
    www.cnt.org/publications/the-new-real-estate-mantra-location-near-pub-
    lic-transportation

9   The Odds of Dying. https://www.livescience.com/3780-odds-dying.html

10 *Factfulness: Ten Reasons We're Wrong About the World—and Why Things
    Are Better Than You Think* by Hans Rosling. ISBN-13: 978-1250107817

11 Weather Fatalities 2017. http://www.nws.noaa.gov/om/hazstats.shtml

12 Travel Statistics. https://travel.state.gov/content/travel/en/passports/after/
    passport-statistics.html

13 Off The Grid: Why Americans Don't Travel Abroad. https://www.
    pastemagazine.com/articles/2016/04/off-the-grid-why-americans-travel-do-
    mestic-instead-1.html

14 The American Diaspora. https://www.esquire.com/news-politics/a5028/
    american-diaspora-1008/

15 *How to Retire Overseas: Everything You Need to Know to Live Well (for Less)
    Abroad* by Kathleen Peddicord. ISBN-13: 978-0525538462

16 *Retirement Without Borders: How to Retire Abroad–in Mexico, France, Italy,
    Spain, Costa Rica, Panama, and Other Sunny, Foreign Places (And the
    Secret to Making It Happen Without Stress)* by Barry Golson. ISBN-13: 978-
    0743297011

17 Genworth Cost of Care. https://www.genworth.com/aging-and-you/
    finances/cost-of-care.html

18 https://www.genworth.com/about-us/industry-expertise/cost-of-care.html

19 About Continuing Care Retirement Communities. https://www.aarp.org/care-
    giving/basics/info-2017/continuing-care-retirement-communities.html

20 http://ltcombudsman.org/about/about-ombudsman

21 *Get Paid for Your Pad: How to Maximize Profit From Your Airbnb Listing* by
    Jasper Ribbers. ISBN-13: 978-0692292815

22 Types of tax to consider: sales, state income, Social Security exemption,
    estate, inheritance, property

CHAPTER 10

Tech Tools For Retirement Success

There is a lot of talk these days about the negative aspects of technology. People worry about cybercrime, kids spending too much time on smartphones, and the feedback loop of political hate on the internet. It tends to make us yearn for simpler times.

But let's not forget all the good that technology has done for us. It has allowed for improvements in medicine, transportation, communication, and information access that have made things easier in ways we tend to take for granted.

"There's an app for that." In recent years, that phrase captured the explosion of technology distilled into applications that help with everything from booking airlines to grocery shopping to tracking how much you walk in a day. Technology can help with every aspect of retirement success that we talk about in this book. There are countless websites and applications that enable you to envision and plan for the retirement you want. You can analyze your financial status, find a home to rent or buy anywhere in the country, find people who share your interests and can help you fulfill your purpose in life, monitor your health, and sort through all of the decisions you face.

In this chapter, we'll explore a number of web-based tools that you can leverage in all areas of retirement happiness planning. We will discuss:

- Finding information

- Managing your finances

- Connecting with people who have relevant experience/ knowledge

- Brainstorming and organizing your thoughts

We realize that our readers possess a broad spectrum of tech savviness, so forgive us if you find some of the upcoming content a little basic. We'll start with common subjects, but toward the end of the chapter, we'll be covering some technology that will probably be new to most of you.

"I checked the serial number of
your laptop. It's a waffle iron."

Finding Information

It has become cliché to say this, but we live in the information age. Almost every word ever recorded by man is available at your fingertips via the internet. Too much information is probably a bigger problem than lack of information at this point. It can be difficult to wade through all the blather, sales pitches, and "fake news" to find useful information on the web.

That said, if you are savvy about searching and put in a bit of time, you can use the internet to gain knowledge on just about any subject imaginable. When discussing searches and offering examples, we will refer to Google. There are other search engines available, but Google is by far the most popular, with 90% of the global market as of this writing.[1]

When it comes to web searching, we have a cautionary tale to share where we saw first-hand the need to be aware of paid ads vs. organic content. Paid ads are, as the name implies, search results where a company has purchased the right to appear at the top of a page. Organic content, on the other hand, is the result of Google's calculations about which websites are most relevant to the user's search.

As first-time authors, one of the things we needed to figure out when we decided to publish this book was: how the heck do you publish a book? So we searched "how to self-publish a book" and began a quest that led to you reading these words right now.

One of the first things we came across when researching book publishing was a service that promised to walk us through the whole process for a seemingly reasonable price. How perfect . . . a guide to this mysterious new world! But we exercised a bit of patience and kept on searching, and reading, and learning.

We eventually learned that the first company we stumbled upon was part of a conglomerate with a poor reputation in the self-publishing community. The company has a history of complaints for shady sales practices, and maintains a variety of different business names that are all part of the same parent entity. We found them in our search not because their service is good, but because they do a great job of marketing themselves on the web. Needless to say, we decided against working with that company.

The lesson we learned is that it often pays to investigate multiple results from a web search, even going to the second or third pages of search results. It also helps to check out forums and organizations dedicated to the subject you are seeking to learn about (more about that later in the chapter). That's how we came across negative information about the company in question.

On the other hand, another of our searches as part of research for this book was on "best places to retire." Through that search, we found a paid listing from a company called the Milken Institute, which provided a report called "Best Cities for Successful Aging."[2] This report is very well researched and informative. It's a real gem of content on the subject, with data provided across a spectrum of criteria including living arrangements, healthcare, financial security, and community engagement. This goes to show that good stuff can sometimes be found among the paid listings; not all of them are clickbait, as discussed in the sidebar. By the time we were wrapping up the book, that web page no longer showed up at the top, so they must not be paying to advertise it any longer (you can find it on the Location page of RetiredHappy.me).

••

Beware of clickbait

When we searched "best places to retire", one of the results was an article called "25 Best Places to Retire" (you might find different results with the same search, depending on who is paying for the ad space at the time of your search).

The Forbes article is an example of "clickbait" . . . instead of linking to a single page, it links to an article whose content is spread over many pages. In fact, each of the 25 Best Places to Retire is listed on a separate page. You have to keep clicking through from one page to the next to get all the info. Why? Because websites typically set their ad prices based on the number of clicks their site receives. So Forbes is paying Google to list their article, in the hopes that someone like you will be interested enough in the article to click through 25 or more pages to read all the info, so they can charge their advertisers a bunch of money based on those clicks.

Clickbait articles are annoying to wade through, and the content is often weak. Of course, it doesn't cost you anything but time and some aggravation to make your way through an article like that, and maybe you'll get some ideas about places you never thought of. That said, we consider that a low-quality search result.

••

In any effort at internet research, you may need to wade through some nonsense to get to the good stuff. Finding good articles and information can be a bit of an Easter egg hunt, so apply some patience to the process.

The Written World at Your Fingertips

As we said, most of what has ever been written can be accessed online in some form. For example, Amazon has become the largest "library" in history. As of the time of this writing, they offer nearly 33 million books![3] Many of them are downloadable in electronic format (more on that in a bit), or as audiobooks.

Naturally, we decided to search for "books on retirement" on Amazon. We knew that we wanted ours to be a guide to the many resources available to people seeking retirement happiness, so we sought the best of what has already been written on the subject. This led us to some of the examples we cited earlier such as *How to Retire Happy, Wild, and Free* and *The New Retirementality*.

The reviews on Amazon, or any other book site, allow you to access the wisdom of crowds. Pay attention to the reviews, as they are a good guide to what is worthwhile. We look for favorable ratings from hundreds of people. If a book has 5-star ratings from 14 people, 7 might be from family and 7 from friends. But as you get up into hundreds of reviews it becomes less likely that the system is being gamed. This is not a hard and fast rule, as newer books will not have many reviews, and there may be some gems that are not well-known. But as a rule of thumb, more is better. We usually look for books with an average rating of four stars or better. An aggregate rating of 5 stars usually only happens in books with few reviews, because there will always be *someone* who doesn't like a book when it has been read by a lot of people.

....

Searches related to themes in this book

Amazon searches, or really any generic web search, can help you find books and other resources related to every topic we've discussed in this book. There are many books related to finding a purpose in life, fitness and diet, finding places to live, and managing finances. We found the following searches useful:

Best places to retire	Retiring overseas
Starting a business	Starting an internet business
Writing a book	Health & wellness
Yoga	Fitness for seniors
Investing	Retirement planning

....

Amazon is just one place you can buy books online. Goodreads is an interactive online community for book fans and a great place to get feedback and reviews from other readers. Barnesandnoble.com is another well-known book site, and you can find many others (by Googling, of course!). There is also Kobo, a site that specializes in e-books and audiobooks.

While some people prefer the feel and experience of a traditional paper book, e-books and audiobooks have become very popular in recent years. Amazon sells books for the Kindle system, which can be read on a tablet or a phone . . . so you can have whatever you're reading in your pocket at all times. If you're reading for research purposes on a Kindle, you can highlight text with your finger and you also have the option to add notes. Then, if you visit read.amazon.com, and sign in with your Amazon password, you'll find all your highlights and notes downloaded so you can review or print them. That's a tool we used quite a bit while writing this book.

Additional e-book options include the Nook from Barnes & Noble, and the Kobo e-reader. Audiobooks can be listened to via apps provided by the bookselling sites. If you read a lot of books, an option to consider is Kindle Unlimited from Amazon, which is a subscription service that allows you to read as many books as you want for no cost beyond the monthly fee (although be aware that not all books are available this way).

Financial Tools

As discussed in previous chapters, there is a lot of information to gather and analyze in terms of planning out your financial future. Even if you use a financial advisor, you may want to do some analysis on your own. There are plenty of online resources available, including:

- Various financial calculators, such as http://www.fncalculator. com/financialcalculator?type=roiCalculator

- Personal Capital, a free online app that (like Mint and Quicken) allows you to aggregate your information from various investment and bank accounts so you can see it all in one place. These "aggregation" software programs offer a variety of budgeting and other tools that help you manage your finances.

- Investor.gov, offered by the U.S. Securities and Exchange Commission, this site provides a variety of tools including an IRA required distribution calculator, a mutual fund analyzer, a program to help calculate retirement income needs, and more.

Check out the Tech Tools[4] page on RetiredHappy.me for a more detailed list of applications available for a variety of topics. It includes those referenced in this book and others.

Leveraging the Combined Brainpower of the Internet

Mobile phones and the internet are allowing people to stay connected with family and friends like never before. But what's interesting from the standpoint of planning your retirement is the possibility of connecting with complete strangers who either share your interests or have knowledge that is useful for you. No matter what challenge or question you face with regard to retirement, someone out there has wrestled with the same issue. And they may have developed a solution that works for you as well. If only you could find them. ...

Online Forums and Discussion Boards

In our search for self-publishing information, we came across two online resources for self-publishing authors. One was KDBoards, a web forum for those who publish for the Kindle device. The other was an organization called the Alliance of Independent Authors, an advocacy group that tracks and rates various providers in the publishing industry. We pass these names along for the benefit of any would-be authors out there. But, more broadly speaking, our experience while researching how to publish this book helps illustrate the power of web forums.

These two sources provided a wealth of information, including warnings about the organization we originally thought about working with. Finding online communities of people who share an interest in a topic is one of the best ways to get good information. To find these, add the word "forum" to whatever you are researching. For example, if you Google "retirement forum" you will probably find one hosted by AARP and several others.

The most useful forums are often the ones with the most traffic, so spend some time figuring out the most popular forums on a particular topic. Most are pretty similar in the way they work. You register by providing an email address and some other information, then you receive an email that allows you to activate your account.

Use multiple email addresses

Whenever you provide your email address to a website, there is always the risk that they will sell your address to spammers, and you will be inundated by sales pitches. That's why many people have an email they use for their personal or business correspondence and another address used solely for online uses (making purchases, communicating with forums, etc.). The alternative emails are sometimes called "burner" emails. Use your burner email address anytime you are signing up with a source that you don't entirely trust or a source you think may lead to lots of spam in your inbox.

Once you register on a forum you can begin posting (either by starting a topic of your own or replying to topics started by others). More importantly—and we suggest you do this before posting questions—you can search the forum for threads that discuss the topic you are interested in. You may find everything you want to know by searching. Otherwise try asking questions of the community. (Be aware that sometimes people get testy if you ask a question that has already been discussed in detail many times on the forum, which is why you should start by searching for existing threads.)

Be careful about providing personal information to forums. Typically, you can make up a pseudonym instead of using your real name. In some cases it might be best to poke around for information without actually registering. You won't be able to post, but depending on the site you might still be able to search for information.

These days there are forums for just about everything. Once you become adept at finding and navigating them, you will have a tremendous ability to gather information by leveraging the opinions and experiences of many other people.

Creativity Tools

As we have emphasized throughout the book, retirement can be a time to reinvent yourself, or move in a new direction. The web is a great place to find new ideas—but those ideas will be useful only if you put them into action. So in this section we're focusing on one tool for finding new ideas (TED Talks), and another called mind-mapping that can help you organize and synthesize all the information you have to process to have a successful retirement.

TED Talks: What are smart people thinking these days?

Early in the book we introduced the concept of TED Talks, and hopefully you have checked out a few by now.

TED is a nonprofit organization that began as a conference in 1984. They have become famous for their library of brief (under 18 minutes) presentations covering an endless array of topics. Some of the brightest minds in the world have used the TED Talk format to share their insights.

In addition to the primary TED Conference, a number of independent events follow the same format under the name "TEDx," adding to the rich array of speakers and subjects.

We encourage you to frequent www.ted.com to keep up with the breadth of accumulated wisdom available there. In fact, watching one TED Talk every day or so is a terrific way to feed your mind in retirement.

In addition to Ted.com, there are blogs (journal-like websites) and podcasts (audio recordings) dedicated to almost any area of interest you might have.

Mind Mapping

Unlike Google and Amazon, the next tool we will talk about is not universally known. It's a technique called "mind mapping" that we have been using as an integral part of our financial planning practice for a number of years now.

Your mind does not make lists. Your memories exist as a web of interconnected experiences, be they sights, sounds, smells or feelings. Each is attached to another, and each is more accessible if you can call upon a related memory as a reminder. Mind mapping is a form of note-taking that is designed to mimic this natural mental structure.

There are two elements to the mind mapping process. The first is brainstorming, where you visually capture on paper or on a computer all of your ideas in a form that is called a map. The act of creating a map stimulates creative thinking, especially if you are careful not to censor yourself. The second element is note taking. Whether you use software or paper, save your maps so you can go back and reference them later. They are a particularly effective way to take notes, and since they are easy to read at a glance, they help you easily recall what you were thinking at the time.

Whether done on a sheet of paper, or with sophisticated software, it is an elegant, simple, and powerful way to record your thoughts. More than just a way to take notes, mind mapping is a method for brainstorming. It encourages and gives structure to creative thinking.

A mind map starts with a central theme, for example, "places to vacation." Then there are branches out to related sub-themes such as various locations or types of vacation. You can then draw additional "twigs" from the branches to describe attributes that relate to each sub-theme. For example, you might put down "cruise" as a category, and then have branches for Caribbean and Panama Canal. Then you could add the category "island," with branches for the Bahamas, Jamaica, and Hawaii. From there you can add descriptive subcategories. For example Hawaii might be described as beautiful but pricey. Eventually you might end up with something like Figure 10.1:

Figure 10.1: Mind Map of Vacation Options

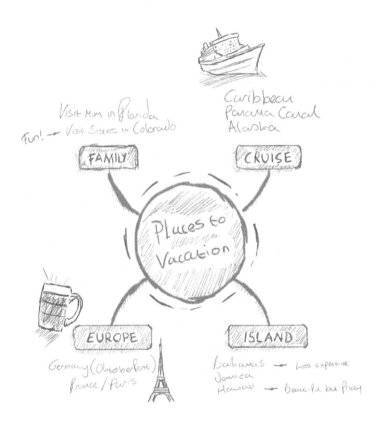

Visit Mom in Florida
Fun! → Visit Sisters in Colorado

FAMILY

Caribbean
Panama Canal
Alaska

CRUISE

Places to Vacation

EUROPE

Germany (Oktoberfest)
France / Paris

ISLAND

Bahamas → Less expensive
Jamaica
Hawaii → Beautiful but Pricey

Using mind maps as To Do lists

With software in particular, you can easily use mind maps as updatable to-do lists. You might have categories such as "house," "charitable," "family," and "finances" that each have sub-branches listing things you need to get done. Simply delete an item once it's done and save the updated map. If you find yourself a busy retiree juggling a lot of different tasks, this can be an easier approach than traditional lists.

It's time to give this a try. Take out a piece of paper, write "places to vacation" in the middle of it, and draw a circle around those words. If you are married, encourage your better half to try this too. You might get a laugh, or maybe even some insight, when you compare notes afterward.

Next, draw some branches out from vacation, and at the end of each line, write a place you might like to visit. Perhaps a certain state or island, a foreign country, national parks, relatives who live somewhere far away, a cruise, a safari, a fishing trip? Think about any trip you would ever like to take. Do not censor yourself! A key element of brainstorming and mind mapping is that you feel free to throw out ideas without applying a filter to your thoughts.

After listing a number of potential vacation ideas, draw twigs out from each and add thoughts or attributes for each. (See our example above.) You can draw additional lines from there to add detail to any of those thoughts. There are no rules or "right" way to do this. Just start with a theme and work outward.

Do not underestimate the power of this simple tactic! Maps can be very basic (which is fine), or you can add colors or doodles to your maps to raise them to the level of artwork. Mind mapping can be a form of journaling, a way to encourage and record creative thought.

We have provided the example of mind mapping for a vacation spot, but there is no limit to the uses for this powerful tool. You can mind map business ideas, places to retire, notes on a book idea (with a branch for each chapter), birthday and holiday gift ideas—any thoughts you want to record and organize. There are a number of books available on this subject, including *Mind Mapping* by Kam Knight.[5]

Creating a mind map can even be a fun and enlightening exercise to do with grandchildren. Try writing their name down as the main topic, then create some categories based on their age and interests. For a pre-teen the categories might be "favorite things to do," "best friends," "goals," "job ideas," and "best things about you." Walk through the exercise with them and have them fill out branches for each category. It's fun and eye-opening . . . and often hilarious. Then, tuck the map away for safe keeping, and repeat the process every year or so. You'll have an interesting and unusual record of their growth over the years.

....

Paper vs. computer

As we've seen from our exercise, mapping can easily be done by hand with paper. Consider using larger sizes of paper such as easel pads if you really want to get into it. But there are also software programs available that make maps very easy to create and store. These programs can be highly sophisticated, capable of creating multilevel maps that are suitable for complex project management. Or they can be very simple (and in some cases free). We recommend the latter for beginners who want to try out mind mapping.

Some examples of software:

- MindMeister—a free program with basic functions (you can later upgrade to a more sophisticated paid version if you wish)

- XMind—another free program with a paid upgrade option

- FreeMind—free program that apparently has a strong support network behind it

- iThoughts—an app for mapping on your phone

- Mindjet—a very robust and sophisticated system, available by monthly subscription (this is what we use in our practice)

....

Retiring in the 21st Century

Preparing for retirement is an important, multifaceted project, and you should treat it as such. Do not underestimate the power of the internet and other modern tools that can help you gather and organize the information you need to plan and make good decisions.

Next we will wrap things up with some steps to follow to bring all of the elements of this book together into one cohesive action plan.

Endnotes

1 Search Engine Market Share Worldwide. http://gs.statcounter.com/search-engine-market-share

2 https://www.milkeninstitute.org/publications/view/852

3 How Many Books Does Amazon Have For Sales? https://www.quora.com/How-many-books-does-Amazon-have-for-sale

4 https://retiredhappy.me/tech-tools-2/

5 *Mind Mapping: Improve Memory, Concentration, Communication, Organization, Creativity, and Time Management* by Kam Knight. ISBN-13: 978-1544840703

CHAPTER 11

The Retirement Happiness Map

People typically give a ton of thought to where they will go to college (a mere four years) or what they will do for a career. But few seem to take a strategic approach to planning all aspects of what could be decades spent in retirement.

The simple exercise that follows is what we think of as "retirement happiness planning." The concept goes beyond traditional retirement planning, which tends to focus on finances, to encompass all the topics we covered in this book. After all, what good is being financially prepared for retirement if your health is a mess, or if you lack any real purpose in life?

So give this process a try, and see where it leads you. If you are part of a couple, you should each create your own map. There will be overlap of course, but there will be differences as well. Comparing your maps can be a fun and enlightening process. If you share finances, you can copy the same data onto the money part of each map.

Preparation

Start by downloading mind map software, because the exercise we are about to walk through is the crafting of a Retirement Happiness Map.

One good free option is XMind, which is available in Windows and iOS versions.

If you prefer a non-tech approach, visit an office supply store and buy yourself a tablet of easel paper. When it comes to creating mind maps, paper can be just as effective as software. And if you like to draw, you may find that creating maps by hand engages your creative side.

It's important to use either software or a very large piece of paper because the mind map you are about to draw is going to be quite big. Each time you add another level of detail, the map gets bigger, and by the time you get three or four levels deep, it's taking up a lot of space (too much for regular paper unless you write very small). So it's best to start with a big piece of paper, or better yet, a software application . . . software never runs out of room.

At this point, you need to put the book down and either download a mind map software package or get yourself a big pad of paper. Don't go any further without one of those, or you will miss out on the entire point of the book.

Go ahead and get a program or big paper—we'll wait.

Welcome back. Now it's time to sketch a Retirement Happiness Map. It won't take a ton of effort and is a guaranteed interesting use of time. Hopefully it will lead to some "aha" moments about how you should approach retirement.

Getting Started

If you are using a software program, take some time to familiarize yourself with the creation of a basic map. Google the name of the program along with "instructions" if you need some guidance. In the case of XMind, you can check out this tutorial[1] on YouTube. If you are using software we recommend printing out a copy of your map when it's complete (so you don't risk losing it if your computer crashes). You can store the map—and subsequent updates—in the personal binder, which we talked about in Chapter 8.

Once you know your way around the software program, start with a blank map and name the central theme "retirement happiness." Or, if you are going old school and are doing this on paper (no shame in that!), write those words down in the middle of the page and draw a circle around them.

Now you are going to put your subtopics in place. From this point forward we won't usually bother describing the computer approach versus the paper approach. Conceptually there is no difference.

Around the central theme put these subtopics (it doesn't matter exactly where each one goes):

- Wellness

- Social Security

- Medicare

- Money

- Location

- Purpose

- Other

You should end up with something like this:

Figure 11.1: Basic Structure of a Retirement Happiness Map

You can use more colors if you want, include doodles (hand-drawn) or insert pictures (software versions). It can be a collage. There are no rules! The idea is to create a visual representation of ideas related to the central theme. In this case, the theme is your quest for happiness in retirement.

Now that you have the basic elements in place, it's time to start drilling down and expanding on each of the sub-subtopics. We will provide instructions for building out your map while at the same time explaining the follow-up tasks that will be required to turn the map into action.

Some of what we are about to describe pertains to pre-retirees. Those already in retirement can customize their maps accordingly and skip certain parts. For example, if you are already receiving Social Security, you might want to leave off the "Social Security" subtopic altogether and just record your income amount in the money section.

Following the example in Figure 11.1, build out the next layer of your map (see Figure 11.2 on the next page). This is the last time we are going to be providing the words for you (other than by way of example). Beyond this level you will begin to customize your map. In each section that follows, we'll describe how to do that (from this point forward we will depict the branches individually so they fit on these small pages).

Figure 11.2: Example of Retirement Happiness Subtopics

Wellness

We start with wellness on purpose. **Remember: taking care of yourself is non-negotiable.** It is the most straightforward way to advance toward your goal of happiness.

If you are not already involved in a regular exercise routine and/or regularly participate in activities that help build muscles, endurance, etc., start with a visit to your primary care physician for a physical and discuss the fact that you intend to begin exercising. Even if you are already exercising regularly but haven't been for a checkup in a while, schedule one soon, and when it's over, schedule the next one a year out. Make routine care part of your wellness plan. Add the date of your next scheduled checkup as a branch on the wellness subtopic. Remember that the structure of Medicare, especially Medicare Advantage, encourages the use of a primary care physician to quarterback your care.

Now, what is your exercise routine going to consist of? Walking, lifting weights, yoga, dance, or aerobics classes are good examples (we encourage variety). Remember to include some strength training as well as cardio. You need both! As a branch of the wellness subtopic on your map, add "My exercise program." Then, as sub-branches, add your activities. If you want, you can include the locations (where you will exercise) as well.

You can also add a branch for diet, listing elements of healthy eating that you intend to make part of your routine.

Next, make a branch for medical providers. Name them and list upcoming appointments.

If there are any other aspects of wellness that you want to include, go ahead and add them. You can always make changes in future iterations of the map (one of the advantages of using software over paper is that it is easy to go back and make updates without having to create a whole new map).

Figure 11.3 shows what the wellness part of a map might look like:

Figure 11.3: Example Wellness Section

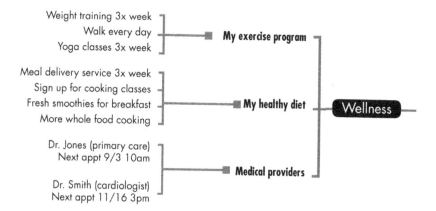

Money

Do you want to work with a financial advisor in retirement or take a do-it-yourself approach? It's a question that will shape how you accomplish some of the other tasks on your map.

If you are already working with a good advisor, write their name down. If you intend to seek a financial advisor and have some options in mind, you could include their names.

If you intend to act as your own advisor, write down the name of the investment platform you intend to use (for example Vanguard, Charles Schwab, or TD Ameritrade).

Your Retirement Happiness Map is not a financial plan, but you can use it to gather data for a plan. When you do put a financial plan together, whether you handle it yourself or use an advisor, you will need two things to get started: your **cash flows** and your **balance sheet**.

Check out the Money and Investing page[2] on RetiredHappy.me for a worksheet you can use to add up your bills. Remember that in addition to routine spending, you need to include periodic costs like vacations, and estimates for unpredictable spending like home repairs. As an alternative to drawing up a budget on paper, you can use software solutions like Mint.com or Quicken, which track your spending over time. Having a strong handle on your spending is important, no matter your level of wealth.

Also, you want to calculate a monthly retirement income figure. Start with the amount you currently receive or expect to get from Social Security each month, plus any potential income from pensions or other fixed sources. For a rough sense of investment income, calculate 4% of the value of your investment portfolio, and divide by twelve to get a monthly figure. If you expect to keep working in some fashion during retirement, you can add expected earned income as well. Remember that these figures are pre-tax (a financial planner, or good financial planning software, will calculate estimated tax implications for you).

Calculate a cash reserve (6 months' worth of expenses is a common rule of thumb, but start with what you currently have set aside). If you know what kind of asset allocation you will use, put that down as well.

You should end up with something like Figure 11.4 (but don't be afraid to add more detail if you'd like):

Figure 11.4: Example Money Section

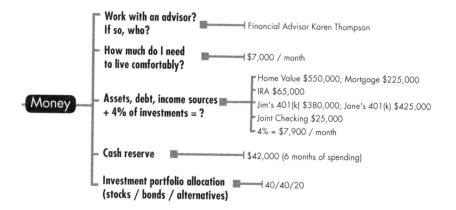

The balance sheet, or statement of net worth, consists of two parts. What you **owe** on one side:

- Mortgages

- Loans

- Credit cards

- Other debts

… and what you **own** on the other:

- Bank accounts

- Investment accounts

- Retirement accounts

- Real estate (house, condo, etc.)

- Other assets

When it comes to other assets, you can get really detailed if you want, but it's not necessary. Things like jewelry, art, and cars may add up to a fair amount of money, but their value won't impact your ability to create income to support your lifestyle. At best they may represent a possible source of funds in an emergency.

Armed with a clear picture of your budget and your balance sheet—along with sources of income such as pensions and Social Security, and investments—you are ready to create a financial plan that analyzes your likelihood of ending up destitute or not.

A financial advisor can create a plan for you. Many will provide one at no additional cost as part of their service model. Some will create a plan for a separate fee. And as we described earlier, there are online tools that will help you create a plan for yourself.

The idea of a financial plan is that it projects your spending and the growth of your assets into the future to see if you are likely to have what you need to live comfortably. And if not, a plan should help determine your options, which basically boil down to making more money, or spending less. The plan can also help you determine how to allocate your investments, bearing in mind that you can expect a higher return by taking on more risk, and vice versa. Of course, in retirement it generally behooves you to minimize risk as best you can.

Understand that because of the variables involved in a financial plan—how much you will spend, the rate of inflation, and your rate of investment return—the projections won't be very accurate beyond a few years, if that. The importance of a financial plan is not in creating highly accurate projections, but rather in giving you a sense of whether or not you are pointed in the right direction at any given time.

Because the plan is just a one-time projection based on current data, you should rerun it periodically to see where you stand. Annually is a good idea, especially early on in retirement and during other periods of change. After you settle into a routine, every couple or few years may suffice. However, you should always keep an eye on your investments to make sure they are performing in line with market conditions, and within range of the projections in your financial plan.

A word of caution about watching your investments, however. Some people watch them obsessively, fretting daily or even hourly over fluctuations in their portfolio. We do *not* recommend that approach. It does little good, can cause stress, and may lead to poor decisions based on short-term circumstances when a long-term outlook (as described in Chapter 4) typically leads to superior results.

Social Security

The first step here is to obtain a copy of your Social Security statement. If you are over age 60, you might have received one in the mail. Otherwise, you can get it here: https://www.ssa.gov/myaccount/.

Next, you want to obtain an analysis that shows what your Social Security income will look like given various claiming strategies (turning on income at age 62 versus waiting until you are older). A financial advisor can provide this, or you can use software:

- SSAnalyze—provided free by Bedrock Capital http://www.bedrockcapital.com/ssanalyze/

- AARP Social Security Benefits Calculator—provided free by AARP http://www.aarp.org/work/social-security/social-security-benefits-calculator.html

- Maximize My Social Security—$40 for an annual license https://maximizemysocialsecurity.com/

Finally, and most importantly, you need to decide on a claiming strategy (and your financial plan should depict that claiming strategy).

Remember that while a majority of Americans turn on their income early, patience often pays off. For married heterosexual couples, it typically makes sense for the wife to turn on early while the husband waits until full retirement age or age 70. For anyone, in the long run there is an advantage to waiting if you end up living a long time.

On your Retirement Happiness map, write down the claiming strategy that you decide upon. It may look something like Figure 11.5.

Figure 11.5: Example Social Security Section

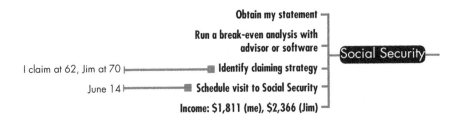

Schedule a visit to your local Social Security office three months ahead of the date that you want to begin receiving your income. Your income will arrive one month after the official activation date, and it takes a couple of weeks to make the activation happen, so you want to get a head start on the process.

Write down the date of your expected visit to your local Social Security office (whether it is scheduled yet or not).

Write down the expected amount of your Social Security income.

Medicare

Eligibility for Medicare begins at age 65, and the enrollment period begins three months prior to that. We recommend that you begin your education and decision making process about one year prior to turning 65. So on the Medicare part of your Retirement Happiness Map, write down "Date to begin Medicare research", and a day around your 64th birthday. Then write down the date that is three months prior to your 65th birthday, when enrollment begins.

As we discussed in Chapter 5, the key first step in figuring out Medicare is to get a good handle on your health status and needs. When the time comes to get started, begin by completing the health assessment available on the Health & Wellness page[3] of RetiredHappy. me. Remember, understanding your health is critical when it comes to choosing the best plan.

Visit Medicare.gov and familiarize yourself with the site. Go to the "Medicare Plan Finder"[4] page and check out the video on the right of the page under the title "Step-by-step overview on how to complete a plan search."

Consider buying *Medicare for Dummies* to serve as a detailed guide.

Once you have a decent handle on how the Medicare system works, you can begin to seek out some professional guidance. If you or your spouse is still employed, check with your HR department to see if they have resources you can tap.

If you are not employed, you can seek out assistance from your State Health Insurance Assistance Program (SHIP). On Medicare.gov there is a drop down box toward the top of the main page titled "Find someone to talk to." You select your state, and the first thing you should see is contact information for the relevant SHIP. Give them a call to seek guidance. But we recommend you do this after completing your health assessment and checking out the video referenced above so that you start your conversation prepared and somewhat knowledgeable.

Another option is to seek a paid consultant or a Medicare insurance broker.

Next, write down "Guidance" and who—if anyone—you plan to turn to for help. Finally, you can begin to make notes about your preferences and your decisions.

The Medicare part of your map should start out looking something like Figure 11.6:

Figure 11.6: Example Medicare Section

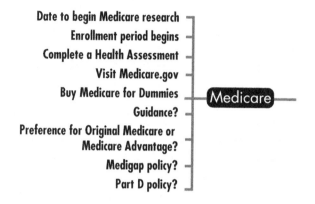

- Date to begin Medicare research
- Enrollment period begins
- Complete a Health Assessment
- Visit Medicare.gov
- Buy Medicare for Dummies
- Guidance?
- Preference for Original Medicare or Medicare Advantage?
- Medigap policy?
- Part D policy?

Medicare

Location

Decisions about location generally fall into three categories: what your priorities are, your options geographically, and a scenario that fits your priorities and options. See Figure 11.7.

Figure 11. 7: Example Location Section

Location

- **Location priorities** — Live somewhere warm, ideally with low taxes
- **Location options** —
  - Florida
  - Arizona
  - Texas
- **Ideal scenario** — Keep an apartment near current home to be near children and grandchildren for part of the year. Buy a house in a warm, fun place as our primary residence.

If you know where you intend to live in retirement (whether in one location or more), write it down. Do you plan to seek out a retirement community of some sort? Write that down if it's one of your goals, and if you have any places in mind, note their names.

If you don't have your location(s) planned out just yet, you should take a moment to describe your ideal scenario. Back in Chapter 9 we provided these examples:

- Buy a home in a retirement community (that includes continuing-care options) near the kids, but rent a place in Florida. Live in Florida more than half the year to take advantage of the favorable tax structure. Later in life, as travel becomes more of a challenge, spend less time in Florida, and eventually give up the rental to live full time in the retirement community.

- Have a regular house and a vacation house while we are working. At retirement, sell the main house and use the proceeds to close out the mortgage on the vacation house, and live there full time.

On your map, describe your ideal scenario. Describe more than one if you aren't exactly sure what you want your living arrangement to look like.

If you have a number of options in mind, list them. Or if you have a number of priorities in mind—weather, proximity to the kids, etc.— list those. Remember, there are no rules to mind mapping. The idea is to record your thoughts in a way that provides clarity.

Purpose

Who are you going to be in retirement? This is what it all boils down to . . . your identity, and your lifestyle. You save and make money to enable the life you want to live. You take care of your mind and your body to help you live well. But what does living well look like? An example of the purpose part of the map can be seen in Figure 11.8.

Figure 11.8: Example Purpose Section

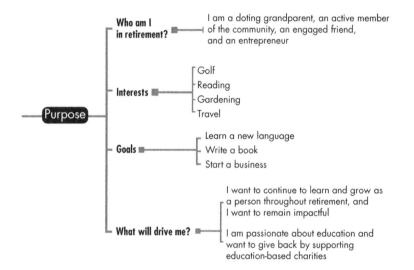

Start with a description of who you are in retirement. For example: "I am a doting grandparent, an active member of my community, an engaged friend, and an entrepreneur." Or perhaps, "I am a philanthropist, a painter, a student, and an explorer." There truly are no limitations. This is an exercise you can repeat again and again, as retirement is an ongoing opportunity for reinvention.

In addition to a self-description, you can add random plans, big and small, well-formed or vague. You can add items that are fun, impactful, or potentially profitable.

- Tour America in a mobile home
- Learn to paint
- Write a book
- Start an internet business
- Improve my golf game
- Spend more time babysitting the grandchildren
- Learn a new language

- Take a memory class
- Volunteer at the library
- Start a charitable foundation
- Start a consulting business
- Run a marathon

Do not censor yourself when it comes to writing down ideas. Include what your passions are, what will drive you. The Retirement Happiness Map is an exercise in free creative thinking.

In fact, retirement in general is an exercise in free creative thinking. This is your last best chance to reinvent yourself. Get after it!

Happiness in Retirement

Nothing in this book, not one word of it, means anything if you don't take positive action steps. Statistically speaking, there is a good chance you won't. Unfortunately the numbers in terms of how many people exercise, or save money, or take other positive, forward-looking actions are not great.

But the fact that you picked up the book in the first place skews the odds in your favor. It suggests that you have intent, that you realize there might be a specific path to retirement happiness and if there is, you want to know about it.

Physical and mental wellness, like the investment markets, involves more probability than certainty. There is so much we don't know and will never know because of lack of data and because of the randomness inherent in matters of health. But you can make good choices based on what is known that can greatly increase your odds of a positive outcome. When it comes to exercise, the right path is particularly easy to describe: exercise, every day. See how easy that was?

With investing, as with wellness, you should avoid wasting time stressing over details that don't necessarily increase your odds. Some people drive themselves crazy trying to figure out when to buy and sell certain stocks, when they can have the same or better chance of a good outcome simply by investing in a fund or an index, and exercising patience. Likewise, too many people worry themselves unnecessarily about picking this diet or that diet, when the best bet is simply to head to the supermarket and stock up in the produce aisle.

"You will want to get a hobby after you retire. Hunting and gathering might be good."

Purpose is about deciding who you are in retirement. Ask yourself that question. Not just once, but again and again. The beauty of retirement is freedom, so who you are right now doesn't have to be who you will be in a year. Life is a constant series of reinventions, and retirement is perhaps the most unfettered opportunity for change.

We have talked about the cyclical nature of many of the factors that relate to happiness. Does being less depressed lead to more exercise, or does exercise help reduce depression? Does losing weight help us feel better, or are we less likely to be heavy if we are happy about ourselves? The answer is yes. Much of wellness and happiness is part of one virtuous cycle.

This is all up to you. Whether you follow our steps exactly, or some variation of your own design, understand that the components of health, financial security, and purpose are universal and elemental.

Don't fall back into retirement as if into an easy chair. Explode into it . . . like you are breaking down a door that leads someplace wonderful. Don't just hope for happiness in retirement, go out and make it happen.

Endnotes

1   https://www.youtube.com/watch?v=zvROXzcyQx4

2   https://retiredhappy.me/money-investing-2/

3   https://retiredhappy.me/health-wellness/

4   https://www.medicare.gov/find-a-plan/questions/home.aspx

Thanks!

We hope you enjoyed *Winning at Retirement.*
Please consider leaving a review of the book on
Amazon.com.

If you would like to learn more about our Financial
Planning practice, visit www.FHBaird.com

We wish you a blissful retirement!

Pat & Kristin

Acknowledgments

We had a lot of help moving this from a crazy idea to the book you just read. We would like to thank our editor, Susan Reynard, who was patient walking rookie authors through the long process of pulling it all together. If *Winning at Retirement* looks professional, we owe that to her.

We would also like to thank the terrifically talented Oliver Bennett, whose artwork adorns these pages. We were hoping for a certain look, and he nailed it. Likewise we appreciate the work of Randy Glasbergen, whose cartoons added a dose of comic relief to these pages.

Thank you, Sarah Moir, our colleague and first editor and fact checker. Also Hilary Graham, who held our hands and guided us through the making of *Winning* from a corporate and marketing perspective (a challenging task). And of course Janet Kelly, who supports us and our clients every single day. Broadly speaking we'd like to thank our employer Baird, a very special place to work and a company that never hesitated to let us follow this dream.

Thanks to our clients, with whom we have formed close relationships over the years. We love the work that we do, and we are grateful to you for letting us do it. This book is for you.

Shannon Henn . . . great job finding that cover shot!

Thanks to the people at CEG Worldwide, who taught us how to use mind mapping in pursuit of holistic financial planning.

Kristin would like to thank her husband, Pete, who believes in her no matter what mountain she would like to climb; and her children, Ryan and Grace, who make life worth living.

Pat would like to thank his wife, Heather, who sat next to him on the couch during much of the writing of this book and encouraged him all along; and his fierce and brilliant daughters, Taylor and Caroline, who inspire him every day.